Student Learning Styles

Diagnosing and Prescribing Programs

W9-BGK-603

National Association of Secondary School Principals
1904 Association Drive, Reston, Virginia 22091

ISBN 0-88210-103-X
Copyright 1979
· All Rights Reserved
National Association of Secondary School Principals
1904 Association Drive
Reston, Virginia 22091

Contents

Contributors

Wesley R. Anderson, principal, Highland High School, Bakersfield, California

S. William Bruce, curriculum coordinator for special programs, Kern County Schools, Bakersfield, California

David P. Cavanaugh, principal, Worthington High School, Worthington, Ohio.

Rita Dunn, professor, department of curriculum and teaching, St. John's University, Jamaica, New York

Kenneth Dunn, superintendent of schools, Hewlet-Woodmere, New York and adjunct professor, St. John's University, Jamaica, New York

Anthony F. Gregorc, associate professor of curriculum and instruction, school of education, University of Connecticut, Storrs, Connecticut

Shirley A. Griggs, associate professor and chairman, department of counselor education, St. John's University, Jamaica, New York

Kenton R. Hill, former principal, York Middle School, York, Nebraska and currently graduate assistant, department of secondary education, University of Nebraska, Lincoln, Nebraska

David E. Hunt, professor, department of applied psychology, Ontario Institute for Studies in Education, Toronto, Ontario, Canada

James W. Keefe, coordinator of research, National Association of Secondary School Principals, Reston, Virginia

Gerald E. Kusler, principal, East Lansing High School, East Lansing, Michigan

Gary E. Price, associate professor, department of counseling and director of the counseling center, University of Kansas, Lawrence, Kansas

Richard M. Restak, practicing neurologist; teacher at the school of medicine, Georgetown University, Washington, D.C.

Armin P. Thies, clinical psychologist, Guilford, Connecticut

Foreword

Understanding the ways students learn is important to good teaching. Yet, until recently student learning style received little attention from most educators. Information about individual patterns of learning was seldom a part of proposals to individualize education.

Numerous efforts, however, have been launched by schools during the past decade to improve individualization of instruction. These efforts ranged from programed learning to flexible scheduling, and from computer-assisted instruction to interactive television. While these programs—and others—enjoyed some success, the general reaction among most practitioners was one of disappointment. No one model appeared to be superior. Student achievement tended to remain constant whether schooling was structured or unstructured. Student attitudes and motivation blew hot and cold depending on the approach.

With the benefit of hindsight, we now see that part of the problem was the tendency to apply a single approach to all students. That is, all students were expected to blossom under independent study or small-group discussion or open classrooms, or whatever. Student learning style challenges this premise and argues for an eclectic instructional program, one based upon a variety of techniques and structures reflecting the different ways that individual students acquire knowledge and skill.

The key, of course, is to understanding these different learning styles, student by student, so that students can better understand their own learning tendencies and schools can design educational structures and materials that respond directly to the individual student's learning tendencies.

This volume describes the pioneering work currently under way in student learning style. It reports upon the research base as well as the experience of practitioners in secondary schools working with learning style. It presents the most complete information available on the theory and practice of this promising approach to improving education.

The individualization of education acquires a richer and deeper meaning when approached through student learning style. Utilizing student proclivities for learning becomes the basis for motivating and instructing students. Differences identified in the ways students learn translate into differences in the ways students receive instruction. We commend its possibilities to your attention.

Appreciation is extended to the authors of this monograph for sharing their research and practice with us, and to NASSP staff member James W. Keefe for coordinating the publication and writing the introductory and concluding chapters.

Owen B. Kiernan
Executive Director
NASSP

Chapter 1

Learning Style: An Overview

James W. Keefe

Learning is a fascinating interactive process, the product of student and teacher activity within a specific learning environment. These central elements of the learning process, in turn, are subject to a wide variation in pattern, style, and quality. In the reality of many schools they seem to operate almost independently of each other. Moreover, the public, the press, and even many in the profession have a generally simplistic view of the relationship between the teaching-learning process and student achievement.

Educators have tended to view instruction and learning as direct correlates. If the one is present to an acceptable degree, the other should naturally follow. If the teacher is working hard, students should learn. If they do not, an earlier generation was inclined to blame the student while the current trend is to hold the teacher (administrator, school) accountable. The reality again is considerably more complex.

Consider these scenarios.

John is a junior at Metro High School. He is a quiet, well-mannered young man, generally accepted by his peers and liked by his teachers. He arrived at the high school with the reputation of being a good student and hard worker. Yet, his grades have gone down every semester since coming to Metro. He is ill prepared to function in the prevailing open, independent study-oriented environment of the high school. He seems to need more structure to achieve, the kind of atmosphere that his junior high school specialized in. His teachers have advised him, given him special attention, even chastized him for a lack of self-direction. He continues to lose ground.

Mary is a seventh grader. Her junior high is the same one from which John graduated. It is a traditional, teacher-centered school of self-contained classrooms and limited curriculum. Everything runs

1

smoothly because structure and order are the dominant controlling mechanisms. Both of Mary's parents are educators who have raised her to be her own person. They have encouraged her to do well in school and have difficulty understanding why she has not responded. Mary always seems to be in trouble. She finds the junior high wearisome and the teachers well meaning but unhelpful. Faculty members seem to have their own agendas. They do not appear to understand Mary's adjustment problems.

Neither student is learning to ability. The fault? Clearly not of the student nor the teachers nor the home alone, but a web of interacting factors. It is a case of student in the wrong place, of unenlightened approaches to instruction.

The School Learning Process

Kurt Lewin noted that "behavior is a function of the person and the environment." Three interacting factors influence the learning process—the student, the instructor, and the school environment. If any of these factors is unsynchronized, the process will falter. John and Mary were unwitting and unwilling victims of a well meaning "snafu." Neither the school nor their parents recognized the mismatch between student style, teacher style, and the predominant learning structure. Their behavior was disfunctional because persons and environment were out of step.

The emphasis in schools has changed from decade to decade. In the 1930s, progressive educators concentrated on the needs of the child. In the 1940s, a nation at war developed a curriculum that was society-centered. In the 1950s and early 1960s, scholars led the way toward a "structure of the (subject) discipline" approach. In the late 1960s and early 1970s the total curriculum came into focus with an emphasis on the humane in schools. As we enter the 1980s, basic skills and educational accountability are the major themes. There is great need for a unifying model amid this continuing search for a better way.

Benjamin Bloom (1976) proposed a significant model of school learning. His theory deals with three important elements: student characteristics, instruction, and learning outcomes. His thesis is that there are three interdependent variables that account for the greatest degree of variance in student learning. These variables are:

1. Cognitive entry behaviors—the extent to which the student has already learned the basic prerequisites to the learning to be accomplished;

2. Affective entry characteristics—the extent to which the student is or can be motivated to engage in the learning process;

3. Quality of instruction—the extent to which the instruction to be given is appropriate to the learner.

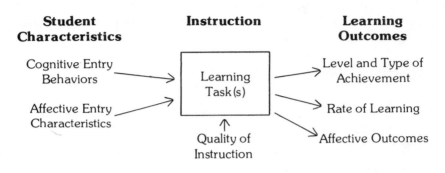

| **Student Characteristics** | **Instruction** | **Learning Outcomes** |

Cognitive Entry Behaviors → Learning Task(s) → Level and Type of Achievement

Affective Entry Characteristics → → Rate of Learning

Quality of Instruction → Affective Outcomes

Figure 1. Bloom's variables in the theory of school learning

Bloom hypothesized that when cognitive and affective entry behaviors and quality of instruction are appropriate, learning will be at a high level and there will be little variation in student outcomes. When student entry characteristics and instructional quality are more variable, learning outcomes will vary accordingly. Variations in level and type of student learning, then, are determined by the students' learning history and the quality of the instructional environment.

Bloom and his colleagues spent a great deal of time researching the effects of student cognitive and affective entry behaviors. There seems to be little doubt that the prior knowledge a student brings to a new learning situation and his attitudes toward self, school, and subject account for the majority of effectiveness in learning. When prior student learning is deficient, the school's job is primarily remedial. When motivation is lacking, counseling and a measure of success are the cures. Only in the area of current instructional quality can the school make its most significant, ongoing contribution. In both instances, early diagnosis and appropriate prescription are the keys to effectiveness.

Experienced educators know that the quality of instruction is greatly influenced by the particular mix of student characteristics, teacher approach, and classroom organization. Bloom's model envisions school learning primarily from the instructional perspective. It deals with prior learning and motivation, the nature of the learning task(s) and indicators of learning effectiveness. It is not directly concerned with the wide variety of approaches that a teacher may utilize in creating a learning environment. Nor does it consider variations in student learning style. Both teaching and learning style, then, are worthy subjects for further conceptualization. Joyce and Weil (1972) developed an excellent classification of teaching styles on the basis of general orientation and purpose. It is the object of this volume to propose a model of student learning styles and to present some selective applications in current research and school practice.

STUDENT LEARNING STYLE

Learning styles are characteristic cognitive, affective, and physiological behaviors that serve as relatively stable indicators of how learners perceive, interact with, and respond to the learning environment.

Because learning is an internal process, we know that it has taken place only when we observe a change of learner behavior of a more or less permanent nature resulting from what has been experienced. The learner behaves differently from before. In a similar manner, we can recognize the learning style of an individual student only by observing his overt behavior. Learning style is a moderating variable, a consistent way of functioning, that reflects the underlying causes of learning behavior. As Gregorc (1979) suggested, "Style appears to be both nature/nurture in its roots. Patterns of adapting to environments are apparently available to us through our genetic coding system... through our environment and culture... (and) within the subjective part of our individual natures." Styles are hypothetical constructs that help to explain the learning (and teaching) process. They are persistent qualities in the behavior of individual learners regardless of the teaching methods or content experienced.

Learning style and cognitive style have often been used synonymously in the literature although they decidedly are not the same. Learning style, in fact, is the broader term and includes cognitive along with affective and physiological styles. This distinction and relationship will become clearer in the course of this discussion.

Elements of learning style appeared in the research literature as early as 1892. Most of that early research (before 1940) concerned the relationship between memory and oral or visual teaching methods. The findings were conflicting, no doubt due in large part to the differences in the populations, learning materials, and test instrumentation that were utilized. Most early researchers were too preoccupied with finding the *one* perceptual mode that would best increase learning or retention. Even before 1900, Cattell and Jostrow attempted to relate differences in perceptual mode to general intelligence and learning performance without success. Vernon, Eysench, and others described perceptual typologies such as analyzers vs. synthesizers and color vs. form reactors.

The term "cognitive style" was coined by Allport in 1937 to refer to a quality of living and adapting influenced by distinctive personality types. In the 1940s, Thurstone and later Guilford identified factors of perceptual speed and flexibility (through the techniques of factor analysis) which they thought were related to personality.

Specific research on cognitive styles was greatly expanded after World War II at Brooklyn College, the Menninger Foundation, and the Fels Institute. Asch and Witkin at Brooklyn College worked with the bipolar trait of "field dependence—independence," the ability of a person to identify a figure against a background field. In time, Witkin and his associates broadened this notion to include "analytic-global" functions and the concept of "psychological differentiation." Holtzman, Gardner, and others at the Menninger Foundation identified a group of cognitive control factors: differentiation vs. undifferentiation, leveling vs. sharpening, equivalence range, tolerance for unrealistic experiences, and flexible vs. constructed control. The Menninger group concentrated on cognitive style as a complexus of cognitive controls. At the Fels Institute, Kagan and his colleagues focused on analytic styles of thinking and problem solving. Research on analytic and non-analytic modes led to the identification of a "reflection-impulsivity" dimension. The reflective person tends to analyze and thoroughly differentiate a complex concept; an impulsive person is inclined to make quick and often erroneous responses.

Although differences in criterion tests used to measure the variables make comparisons a bit shaky, Davis (1967) saw a similar active-passive dimension in the work of the Brooklyn, Menninger, and Fels groups, as follows:

Active Analysis		*Passive (Global) Acceptance*
Field independence	(Witkin)	Field dependence
Differentiation	(Gardner)	Undifferentiation
Reflection	(Kagan)	Impulsivity

The consideration of cognitive style has widened since 1960 to include selection strategies (scanning and focusing), open/closed mindedness, memory or retention styles, risk taking vs. cautiousness, and sensory modality preferences (kinesthetic, visual, and auditory).

Current efforts to explain the underlying processes of learning and teaching reflect two lines of research. One group is working with *applied models of learning style.* This group, represented by David Hunt, Joseph Hill, and Rita and Kenneth Dunn, is concerned about the multi-dimensional implications of learning style. Interview techniques or self-report questionnaires are utilized to allow students to identify their own perceptions of their characteristic traits. The other line of research retains a strong preference for the *cognitive* style dimension. A good illustration is the model developed by McKenney and his associates (1974) at the Harvard Business School. This model is bi-dimensional rather than simply bipolar. For McKenney, human information processing has two dimensions: information gathering (preceptive vs. receptive) and information evaluating (systematic vs. intuitive). Thus far, the model has been applied primarily to the managerial decision-making process.

Aptitude-Treatment Interaction (ATI) analysis, following Cronbach and others, is a systematic attempt to relate individual differences in aptitude, including aspects of cognitive and affective style, to instructional method. The ATI hypothesis is that aptitudes in the general sense—"whatever makes a person ready to learn rapidly in a particular situation"—can and does interact with instructional treatment or method to affect student learning performance (Cronbach and Snow, 1977). Berliner and Cohen prefer the term "trait-treatment interaction," regarding "trait" as less restrictive than "aptitude." Hunt suggests "person-environment interaction." In any event, this developing line of research offers great hope for unifying the efforts of learning style and cognitive style advocates in the compass of a single theory of the school learning process.

APPLIED MODEL OF THE SCHOOL LEARNING PROCESS

There is every indication that a consensus is developing in the applications of learning style theory and research. Major impetus in this direction has come from groups concerned with improving and individualizing instruction and those supporting the cause of the physically handicapped and learning disabled. What is probably needed more than anything else at this point of development is an applied model of the school learning process, including the dimensions of learning style.

Figure 2 outlines the components of a practical model of the school learning process as suggested by aptitude or trait-treatment interaction studies, learning-teaching style research, and particularly the mastery

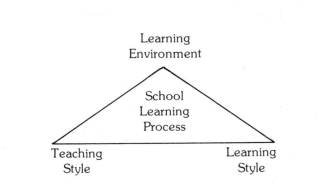

Figure 2. The School Learning Process

learning research of Bloom and his associates. In this model, the school learning process is viewed as an interaction between the methodological environment, the approach to teaching, and the traits of individual learners. One could readily visualize these themes as expansions of Bloom's concept of instructional quality. Each component of the model is currently the object of major theoretical research and a number of practical applications. The classroom learning environment was the focus of countless innovations for individualizing instruction in the 1960s and early 1970s. Several major projects graced the national scene, including Individually Prescribed Instruction (IPI) and Individually Guided Education (IGE) at the elementary level and Project PLAN (Program for Learning in Accordance with Needs) and the NASSP Model Schools Project (MSP) at the secondary level. The latter has seen several spinoffs, notably the Learning Environments Consortium (LEC) in the western part of the United States and Canada. IGE/Secondary has expanded the thrust of that system to the middle and secondary levels. Research attempting to relate learning resources and methods to student performance criteria has accompanied all these efforts.

Teaching style is understood in the sense advanced by Joyce and Weil (1972). These authors emphasize that teachers may adopt or adapt a wide range of options to their own unique local situations. The formality here is on models of teaching that are well conceived and highly communicable. Joyce and Weil identify families or groups of teaching models derived from four sources: (1) Social interaction, (2) Information-processing, (3) Personal (personality) sources, and (4) Behavior modification approaches. In actual application, these groups of teaching models are interrelated and may result in learning schemes that are quite similar.

Learning style, the subject of the present volume, is conceived of in three dimensions: 1) cognitive style, 2) affective style, and 3) physio-logical style. It is important that we consider each of these elements in some detail.

Cognitive Styles

Cognitive styles are "information processing habits representing the learner's typical mode of perceiving, thinking, problem solving, and remembering." (Messick, 1969) As our brief review of the learning style movement has indicated, the vast majority of research on per-sonality-related learning variables has been in the area of cognitive style. Each learner has preferred ways of perception, organization, and retention that are distinctive and consistent. These characteristic dif-ferences are called cognitive styles. In the broad language of ATI, styles are aptitudes or traits of the individual, functioning personality.

Cognitive styles are related to, but different from, intellectual abil-ities. The latter are usually referred to as general intelligence, mental ability, scholastic ability, IQ, or even aptitude. There are notable dif-ferences between styles and abilities (Messick, 1976). Abilities deal with the *content* of cognition; they tell *what* kind of information is being processed by what operation in what form. Styles, on the other hand, illustrate the *process* of cognition: they tell *how* information is being processed. Abilities measure specific innate capacities and are value directional—more of an ability is better than less. Styles are con-trolling mechanisms concerned with manner or preference of perform-ance and are value differentiated—each extreme style has learning-adaptive value in differing circumstances.

There is some common ground between abilities and styles. For example, cognitive fluency and flexibility (abilities) and complexity vs. simplicity (styles) appear to fall somewhere between ability and style. Both are basically bipolar with differentiated value attached to the extremes depending on the circumstances, yet greater value is ordinarily attached to one pole of the dimension than to the other. Similarly, sex-related learning differences probably are abilities but are perceived as styles.

Messick (1976) lists more than 20 dimensions of cognitive style that are derived from experimental research. Some of these elements are straightforward in their meaning and implication; others are very complex. It is possible to organize the style dimensions in a general way as they touch on either reception or concept formation and re-tention. Reception styles are concerned with the perception and analy-sis of data. Concept formation and retention styles deal with hypo-thesis generation, problem solving, and memory processing.

RECEPTION STYLES

1. *Perceptual modality preferences*—preferred reliance on one of the three sensory modes of understanding experience. The three modes are kinesthetic or psychomotor, visual or spatial, and auditory or verbal. Preference seems to evolve from kinesthetic in childhood to visual and eventually verbal in later years. There are, of course, many exceptions to this. In adults, all three modes function cooperatively with a usually discernible preference for one or the other. (Brunner; Sperry)

2. *Field independence vs. dependence*—analytical as opposed to a global way of experiencing the environment. Independents perceive things as discrete from their background field, while dependents tend to be influenced by any embedding context. This style has perhaps been the subject of more research than any other. (Witkin)

3. *Scanning*—differences in the way individuals deploy attention. Attention may be broad or narrow and a person's style may be to scan or focus. The scanning or extensiveness dimension has received more attention from researchers than the focusing or intensity element. (Holzman; Brunner)

4. *Constricted vs. flexible control*—individual differences in susceptibility to distraction and distortion in tasks with conflicting cues. The constricted style is more susceptible to distraction while the flexible style tends to concentrate on the task at hand. (Gardner et al.)

5. *Tolerance for incongruous or unrealistic experiences*—readiness to accept perceptions at variance with conventional experience. A high tolerance style reflects a willingness to accept experiences that vary markedly from the ordinary or even the truth. Low tolerance implies a preference for conventional ideas and reality orientation. (Gardner et al.)

6. *Strong vs. weak automatization*—the capacity to perform simple repetitive tasks. Relative skill in performing simple tasks has been found to run contrary to relative skill in perceptual analysis, suggesting an intra-individual style of *automatization vs. restructuring*. A strong automatization style appears to concentrate on the obvious properties of a task, ignoring the detail that restructuring requires. (Broverman)

7. *Conceptual vs. perceptual*—the capability to perform novel or difficult tasks. Conceptually dominant persons exhibit greater facility for conceptual behaviors and less for perceptual-motor ones. Perceptual-motor dominant individuals display the opposite pattern. (Broverman)

CONCEPT FORMATION AND RETENTION STYLES

1. *Conceptual tempo* —individual differences in the speed and adequacy of hypothesis formulation and information processing on a continuum of *reflection vs. impulsivity*. Impulsives tend to give the first answer they can think of even though it is frequently incorrect. Reflectives prefer to consider alternate solutions before deciding and to give more reasoned responses. (Kagan)

2. *Conceptualizing styles* —individual differences in approach to concept formation. *Conceptual differentiation* refers to the tendency to conceive of things as having many properties rather than a few. *Compartmentalization* is the inclination to place concepts in discrete, even relatively rigid, categories. The chief conceptualizing bases are the use of thematic or functional relations among stimuli *(relational conceptualizing)*, the analysis of descriptive attributes *(analytic-descriptive conceptualizing)* or the inference of categorical membership *(categorical-inferential conceptualizing)*. (Kagan; Gardner; Messick and Kogan)

3. *Breadth of categorizing* —preference for broad or narrow range in establishing conceptual categories. The broad categorizer likes to include many items and lessen the risk of leaving something out. The narrow categorizer prefers to exclude doubtful items and lessen the probability of including something deviant. (Brunner; Messick and Kogan)

4. *Cognitive complexity vs. simplicity* —differences in number of dimensions utilized by individuals to construe the world. A high complexity style is multidimensional and discriminating, attuned to diversity and conflict. A low complexity style prefers consistency and regularity in the environment. The former is more effective in processing dissonant information; the latter, in reconciling consonant experience. Harvey and his colleagues refer to this dimension as *abstract vs. concrete*. (Bieri; Harvey; Scott)

5. *Leveling vs. sharpening* —individual variations in memory processing. Levelers tend to blur similar memories and to merge new precepts readily with previously assimilated experience; they tend to over-generalize. Sharpeners are inclined to magnify small differences and to separate memory of prior experiences more easily from current data; they tend to over-discriminate. Kogan believes that this style could have particularly important implications for education. (Holzman; Gardner)

Affective Styles

The second dimension of learning style encompasses those dimensions of personality that have to do with attention, emotion, and valuing. The psychology of motivation deals with the processes of arousal, expectancy, and incentive. Arousal describes the general level of attention and responsiveness of an organism. Optimum attention is ordinarily an intermediate level between boredom and excitement. Arousal encompasses traits such as curiosity, exploratory behavior, boredom, anxiety, and frustration. Expectancy is the subjective certainty that a particular outcome will follow a particular act, that something will or will not occur. Anticipated satisfaction or emotional preference (valence) is associated with expectancy. The strength of a person's action is a product of both expectancy and valence. A learner strives for whatever he desires greatly (valence) and has high hope of success (expectancy). The "motive to achieve" is an example of the expectancy of finding satisfaction (valence) in mastering challenging tasks. Incentives are the consequences of learning. They may be actual or symbolic rewards. Positive and negative reinforcers and punishment may be viewed as incentives.

Motivation is a product of arousal, expectancy, and incentive. *Affective learning styles are these same motivational processes viewed as the learner's typical mode of arousing, directing, and sustaining behavior.* As with cognitive style, affective style is a hypothetical construct. We cannot directly observe affective style, only *infer* it from a person's interaction with the environment. And, there are many motivational processes. Affective learning style is a product of these intersecting and interacting forces resulting in relatively consistent behavior for a given learner in a given environment. Individual motivational responses may vary but the learner's affective style will remain fairly stable over any reasonable period of time.

Obviously a large subjective component exists in all of this. Ball (1977) put it succinctly:

> A teacher sees a student as motivated if the student wants to do, and does, those things the teacher thinks the student should do. By the same token, a student is seen by the teacher as unmotivated if the student will not do, or has to be made to do, those things that a teacher thinks the student should do.

Affective style is the result of a network of motivational processes that are subject to a wide variety of influences. The learner is affected by the cultural environment, parental and peer pressures, school influences, and personality factors. Values are involved. Not every student can be successful in every learning environment because accustomed habits/may prove to be at odds with the school values. Diagnosis of affective learning style is critical, then, to the effective functioning of the school learning process.

It is useful to classify the many dimensions of affective style according to some general scheme. We will use the elements of attention and expectancy/incentive as the basis for our classification. Placement in the categories is by no means definitive; there is certainly some conceptual overlap among the styles. The basis for determination is the dominant focus of the affective trait(s) emphasized in the style.

ATTENTION STYLES

1. *Conceptual level*—a broad development trait characterizing how much *structure* a student requires in order to learn best. CL is "based on a developmental personality theory that describes persons on a developmental hierarchy of increasing conceptual complexity, self-responsibility, and independence." (Hunt, 1977) A low conceptual level style indicates the need for high structure; high CL, that the learner requires less structure. Conceptual level is a broad trait and is classified here mainly because of its developmental implications. Closely related to it are *responsibility*, the capacity of students to follow through on a task without direct or frequent supervision, and *need for structure*, the amount and kind of structure required by different individuals. (Hunt, Dunn and Dunn)

2. *Curiosity*—differences in attraction to the novel or adventuresome aspects of the environment. Curiosity can be seen as exploratory behavior, in reactions to changes or simply the need for change, and in the desire to escape boredom. Not all psychologists are in agreement about the nature of curiosity, but it does seem to grow out of the perception of some kind of discrepancy in the environment. (Berlyne; Montessori)

3. *Persistence or perseverance*—variations in learner's willingness to labor beyond the required time, to withstand discomfort and to face the prospect of failure. High persistence is characterized by the disposition to work at a task until it is completed, seeking whatever kind of help is necessary to persevere. A low persistence style results in short attention span and the inability to work on a task for any length of time. (Carroll; Dunn and Dunn)

4. *Level of anxiety*—describes the individual's level of apprehension and tension under stress conditions. The highly anxious are tense and

worried; the unanxious are "cool" emotionally. A low anxious learner performs better when challenged by a difficult task, particularly when his performance will be evaluated. A high anxious learner performs less well under these same conditions. There is some evidence that high intelligence learners may profit more from anxiety than the less able. (Alpert and Haber; Spielberger)

5. *Frustration tolerance*—individual differences in thwarting behavior in the face of conflict or disappointment. The learner low in frustration tolerance is more likely to extend effort in a conflict situation—to accept the challenge. (Waterhouse and Child)

EXPECTANCY AND INCENTIVE STYLES

1. *Locus of control*—variations in individual perceptions of casuality in behavioral outcomes on a continuum of *internality vs. externality.* The internal person thinks of himself as responsible for his own behavior, as deserving praise for successes and blame for failures. The external person sees circumstances beyond his control, luck, or others as responsible for his behavior. There is some evidence that a greater sense of internality can be developed. (Rotter; Crandall, Kratkovshy and Crandall)

2. *Achievement motivation*—individual differences in patterns of planning and striving for some internalized standard of excellence. Individuals with high achievement motivation are interested in excellence for its own sake rather than for any rewards it may bring. They set their goals carefully after calculating the success probability of a variety of alternatives. This style is also called *need for achievement* (n-Ach). This is probably the most thoroughly researched affective style. (McClelland; Alschuler)

3. *Self-actualization*—differences in personal striving for adequacy. Maslow and other humanistic psychologists view life as a "continual series of choices for the individual in which the main determinant of choice is the person as he already *is* (including his goals for himself, his courage or fear, his feeling of responsibility, his ego-strength or "willpower," etc.)." The more actualized person has greater feelings of "adequacy." (Maslow)

4. *Imitation*—the tendency to repeat actions that appear desirable in a given situation. The young, in particular, identify with role models and tend to imitate what they say and do. The occurrence of imitative behavior seems to depend on the perceived personality of the model, the personality of the learner and the interaction between the two factors. (Bandura; Fisher)

5. *Risk taking vs. cautiousness*—individual differences in a person's willingness to take chances to achieve some goal. Risk takers prefer low probability-high payoff alternatives; cautious persons like high probability-low payoff ones. (Kogan and Wallach)

6. *Competition vs. Cooperation*—tendency of individuals to be motivated more by rivalry or by the sharing of experience. In solving various problems, Deutsch found cooperative *groups* superior in almost every respect, but the group is not necessarily any more successful than the best problem solver in it. The highly competitive have a strong compulsion to win; the highly cooperative, a strong need to agree and support. (Maccoby; Marquart)

7. *Level of aspiration*—variations in learner perception of past successes and failures in relation to subsequent school performance. Bloom and his colleagues term this style *academic self-concept.* Past successes tend to develop modest self-confidence while failure can lead either to despair or to an unrealistic optimism born out of defeat. Those who often fail tend to develop a mind set ranging from a lowered level of expectancy to the need to discredit the evidence of failure. (Bachman; Bloom et al.)

8. *Reaction to reinforcement*—individual differences in response to reward and punishment. A positive reinforcer is some kind of reward (e.g., praise, prizes, money). A negative reinforcer is the removal of an unpleasant state or event (e.g., threat of punishment, scolding). Punishment is the removal of reward and the addition of an aversive stimulus. Generally speaking, students are motivated by reinforcement and variable in response to punishment. (Skinner; Solomon)

9. *Social motivation*—differences in value-based behavior based on variations in social and racial/ethnic world view. Learners not only vary in socio-economic background, in cultural determinants and value codes, and in peer-group conformity but are variously affected by the standards and expectations of these groups. Esthetic sense, for example, is strongly influenced by social and ethnic background. Value systems arise out of family, school, and peer-group influences. Differences in social motivation may derive from one or a combination of determinants. (Hill; Bennett)

10. *Personal interests*—patterns of choice among alternatives that do not seem to result from external pressures. All else being equal, when an individual has an interest in something, he is likely to favor it over its alternatives. High interest will incline a learner toward an activity; low interest, away from it. (Witty)

Physiological Styles

The final grouping of learning styles arises directly from a consider-ation of the customary functioning of the human body. *Physiological styles are biologically-based modes of response that are founded on sex-related differences, personal nutrition and health, and accustomed reaction to the physical environment.* Physiological factors are among the most evident influences in the process of school learning. The student who is hungry, ill, or a victim of continuing malnutrition be-haves differently than the youngster who is healthy. Boys and girls respond differently in certain learning situations.

The small number and more obvious nature of the physiological factors make any additional basis for classification unnecessary.

1. *Masculine-feminine behavior*—variations in typical brain-behavior responses of boys and girls. Researchers agree that males generally are more aggressive, sensitive to spatial (visual) relations and (per-haps) to mathematical processes. Girls are more verbal and excel in fine muscular control. The sexes display differing attentional mechan-isms and widely varying interest patterns. Sex-related differences may be more closely akin to abilities than to style and they are cer-tainly related to brain hemispheric dominance. In any case, their per-vasive influence makes inclusion imperative. (Maccoby and Jacklin)

2. *Health-related behavior*—individual response differences result-ing from the physical imbalance of malnutrition, hunger, and disease. Dunn and Dunn refer to an aspect of this style as *intake*. There are no widely accepted measures of these factors and the many potential implications for learning can only be surmised because of the clumsi-ness of the available methodology. Yet it is clear that the differences do exist. (Cravioto; Dunn and Dunn)

3. *Time rhythms*—individual variations in optimum learning patterns depending on the time of day. Some persons perform best in the morning; others in the afternoon or evening. (Dunn and Dunn)

4. *Need for mobility*—differences in learner need for change in posture and location. This dimension may be both age and sex-linked since younger learners and males generally require more mobility. (Dunn and Dunn)

5. *Environmental elements*—individual preference for, or response to, varying levels of light, sound, and temperature. Few learners are greatly bothered by light variations but many find it hard to work with distracting noise levels, and wide temperature variations affect almost everyone. (Dunn and Dunn)

Summary

The school learning process is a consequence of learning environment, teaching style, and student learning style. Reform efforts of the 1960s and 1970s have moved the purposes and importance of individualized instruction to the forefront of American education. Joyce and Weil and others have begun to investigate different models of teaching style. Learning style has received major attention in the synthesizing work of McKenney, Hill, Hunt, and the Dunns. The McKenney model is based primarily on the cognitive style research of Witkin and Bruner. Hill's cognitive style mapping is an applied model developed as part of his larger framework of "educational sciences." Hunt's conceptual level matching model profiles the degree of structure needed by learners. The Dunns' work has been synergistic, drawing together cognitive, affective, and physiological styles from research and school applications.

Learning style emerges from this picture as a key element in the movement to make learning and instruction more responsive to the needs of individual students. We have defined learning styles in this larger context as characteristic cognitive, affective, and physiological behaviors that serve as relatively stable indicators of how learners perceive, interact with, and respond to the learning environment. Cognitive styles are information-processing habits; affective styles, motivational processes; physiological styles, biologically-based response modes.

It is crucial to emphasize here that, practically speaking, not all the elements of learning style can be applied simultaneously. Even if educators wished to do so, the present state of the research and testing instrumentation would make it impossible to evaluate students on all these characteristics. Some of the styles have no generally acceptable testing techniques and others are still vague enough that much more investigation is needed. What is important at this point is that the reader have a good grasp of the concept of *learning style* and how the cognitive, affective, and physiological dimensions are related to it.

The following chart summarizes the major cognitive, affective, and physiological styles. Inclusion of a style is grounded on the current level of significance of its research, its conceptual importance, or its practical utility. Many styles have been omitted either because their validity is uncertain, their application is questionable, or their meaning is subsumed in another style that is listed. A few styles, conceptually debatable, have been included for their practical significance. Styles that seem to have the greatest implication for improving the learning process have been marked with an asterisk.

The chapters that follow explore a number of applied learning style models or discuss in some detail a specific aspect of learning style research or its school-based application.

STUDENT LEARNING STYLE

Cognitive Styles

Reception Styles

* Perceptual modality
   preferences
* Field independence vs.
   dependence
   Scanning
   Constricted vs. flexible
   control
   Tolerance for incongruous
   or unrealistic experiences
   Strong vs. weak automatization
   Conceptual vs. perceptual-
   motor dominance

Concept Formation and Retention Styles

* Conceptual tempo
   Conceptualizing styles
   Breadth of categorizing
   Cognitive complexity vs.
   simplicity
* Leveling vs. sharpening

Affective Styles

Attention Styles

* Conceptual level
   Curiosity
   Persistence or perseverance
   Level of Anxiety
   Frustration tolerance

Expectancy and Incentive Styles

* Locus of control
* Achievement motivation
   Self-actualization
   Imitation
   Risk taking vs. cautiousness
   Competition vs. cooperation
   Level of aspiration
   Reaction to reinforcement
* Social motivation
   Personal interests

Physiological Styles

* Masculine-feminine behavior
   Health-related behavior
   Time rhythms
   Need for mobility
   Environmental elements

Chapter 2

Learning/Teaching Styles: Their Nature and Effects

Anthony F. Gregorc

The whole is greater than the sum of the parts. This is an apt summary of the emerging concept of learning and teaching styles. To date, much that has been discussed in educational literature has been in regard to parts. Current investigations, however, are revealing "hidden" interrelationships and a glimpse at the whole. The purpose of this chapter is to share some observations and inferences about this important new area of inquiry.

WHAT IS LEARNING STYLE?

Learning style, from a phenomenological viewpoint, consists of distinctive and observable behaviors that provide clues about the mediation abilities of individuals. In operational terms, people through their characteristic sets of behavior "tell" us how their minds relate to the world and, therefore, how they learn. These characteristic sets reflect specific mind-qualities that persist even though goals and content may change.

Mind-qualities emerge as dualities—abstract and concrete perception, sequential and random ordering, deductive and inductive processing, and separative and associative relationships. Everyone has all of these qualities, but most people also have innate tendencies that "tip" toward one aspect of a duality rather than the other; i.e., we are more concrete than abstract or more sequential than random.

These mind-qualities serve as mediators as we learn from and act upon our environment. They are vital to our survival in the three-dimensional world. Physically (i.e., phenomenologically), they are manifested as behavior and register in our conscious minds as preferred means of learning and teaching. The behaviors and related

19

preferences, in turn, allow us to identify styles through observation, interviews, and paper-and-pencil instrumentation.

EXAMPLES OF STYLE

An interest in helping teachers to understand the complexity of human learning and the need for careful learning diagnosis and prescription led us several years ago to begin to investigate the behavior of learners within the classroom. We observed and interviewed students and adults about the way they accumulated and reacted to facts, principles, attitudes, and skills. The resultant data clearly revealed that there is a duality in learning preference. People learn both through concrete experiences and through abstraction. Further, both of these modes have two subdivisions, sequential and random preference.

Abstract (A)/ Concrete (C) and Sequential (S)/ Random (R) proclivities have been found to combine in several styles. As we assessed behavior, we discovered that these sets of dualities merged to form four distinct learning patterns. These are:

Concrete Sequential (CS)

Concrete Random (CR)

Abstract Sequential (AS)

Abstract Random (AR)

We found that everyone exhibits all four patterns to some degree—however, most people exhibit "tippings" toward one or two.

The following examples[1] of behaviors and preferences are offered to aid understanding:

The Concrete Sequential Learner (CS)

The concrete sequential learning preference is characterized by the propensity to derive information through direct, hands-on experience. CS learners exhibit extraordinary development of their five senses. They appreciate order and logical sequence of the if-then, premise-conclusion variety. They like touchable, concrete materials. In a biology class, a plaster model handled by the teacher would be insufficient for these learners. They want to have the real thing to take apart themselves.

---

1. Gregorc, Anthony F., and Ward, Helen B., "Implications for Learning and Teaching—A New Definition for Individual," *NASSP Bulletin,* Vol. 61, No. 406, Feb. 1977, pp. 20-23.

The CS learners prefer step-by-step directions when confronted with a learning situation. They not only look for directions but they follow them. They like clearly ordered presentations and a quiet atmosphere.

The Concrete Random Learner (CR)

The concrete random learning preference is characterized by an experimental attitude and accompanying behavior. CR learners get the gist of ideas quickly and demonstrate the ability to make intuitive leaps in exploring unstructured problem-solving experiences. Sometimes they also have insights and make leaps in structured situations. Then they are chided for not showing their steps or for jumping to conclusions.

Concrete random learners utilize the trial-and-error approach in acquiring information. They do not like cut-and-dried procedures that deny them opportunities to find answers in their own ways. They do not respond well to teacher intervention in their dependent efforts. They work well independently or in small groups.

The Abstract Sequential Learner (AS)

The abstract sequential learning preference is characterized by excellent decoding abilities with written, verbal, and image symbols. AS learners have a wealth of conceptual "pictures" in their minds against which they match what they read, hear, or see in graphic and pictorial form. They possess and like to use reading, listening, and visual translation skills. A symbol or picture is worth a thousand words to them.

These learners prefer a presentation that has substance, is rational, and is sequential in nature. They are able to extract main ideas from a logical presentation. They learn well from authorities and like vicarious experiences.

The Abstract Random Learner (AR)

Abstract random learners are distinguishable by their attention to human behavior and a capacity to sense and interpret "vibrations." They are attuned to nuances of atmosphere and mood. They associate the medium with the message and tie a speaker's manner, delivery, and personality to the message being conveyed. In doing so, they evaluate a learning experience as a whole.

Abstract random learners prefer to receive information in an unstructured manner and therefore like group discussions, activities which involve multi-sensory experiences, and busy environments.

They prefer freedom from rules and guidelines. They seem to gather information and delay reaction; they organize material through reflection to get what they want.

Additional studies have shown that other dualities such as deductive/inductive processing are manifest in behaviors like test taking, question-and-answer patterns, self-directedness, and various forms of group work.

SOURCES OF STYLE

Learning styles emerge from inborn, natural predispositions or proclivities. They need to be recognized, brought out, encouraged, unfolded, developed, and disciplined. It is abundantly clear also that individuals can learn certain stylistic behaviors and add them synthetically to their repertoire. For example, a "natural" Concrete Random (CR)-Oriented learner with a low CS "tipping" may find himself in an environment which demands the CS ability for handling precise details and for direct task orientation. He can "learn" the CS sets of behaviors and skills. He will learn them, however, only in terms of his limited CS capacity and his willingness to work at practicing the behaviors. He will not be as smooth or efficient as a "natural" with a major CS proclivity.

An obvious implication of this finding is that individuals are capable of using their minor proclivities to varying extents and that development of these proclivities is necessary because of the multivariate demands from our environment. A deeper implication is that any given environment may make comfortable demands upon the mind-qualities of one person while placing frustrating and painful burdens upon another.

LEARNING STYLE AND TEACHING STYLE

Phenomenologically, teaching style consists of a teacher's personal behaviors and the media used to transmit data to or receive it from the learner. Teacher behaviors and media use place demands upon *both* the teacher and the learner to align their mind-qualities.

We have found that a teacher who has tight behavioral objectives, starts classes at the bell, gives a true/false test every Friday, uses seating charts for attendance purposes, declines to meet with students after school, and requires 490 points for a grade of "A," is placing certain demands upon a learner. These teacher behaviors appeal to persons with CS-type preferences, dominant deductive processing abilities, and a separative relationship orientation.

Some learners align with ease. Others have difficulty and show reluctance to align, in part, because they are unsure of themselves. Still others do not adjust well at all and are inclined to ask the teacher for options. The latter probably need assistance in tipping toward the CS orientation but may not perform well irrespective of the time and energy devoted to "stretching" in that direction. As one young man told us, "I just can't learn in that environment."

The media chosen by a teacher also are related to mind-qualities. We have found, for example, that concrete/sequential (CS)-oriented learners report preferences for workbooks, manuals, demonstration teaching, programmed instruction, hands-on materials, and well-organized field trips. The abstract/random (AR)-oriented learner shows a predilection for movies, group discussions, short lectures accompanied by question/answers and discussion, and television. The abstract/sequential (AS) learner feels the need for extensive reading assignments, substantive lectures, audio tapes, and analytical "think-sessions." Finally, concrete/random (CR) learners like games and simulations, independent study projects, problem-solving activities, and optional reading assignments.

STYLES AND STRESS

All teaching approaches appear to cause learners some degree of stress. This is understandable inasmuch as instruction may challenge the learner's complex and delicate mind-qualities and his ability and willingness to adapt. The stress can be indiscernible. Or it can be subtly destructive.

It is clear from our interviews that some behaviors and techniques have adverse effects upon certain learners. Forcing a minor AS (i.e., a poor reader) to read 40 pages of a textbook each night, or demanding that all students critique the same movie can provide transient benefits such as passing a test or responding orally in class. But, there can be delayed reactions.

The learner may associate pain with extensive reading or with the movies in these cases. The media readily become a message of pain and of potential failure, irrespective of the underlying goal or the meaningful content of the book or movie. In some situations, the learner may link the forced reading with an entire subject matter discipline. He may associate protracted reading with U.S. History, or movies with English, or true/false tests with physics. Indeed, some elementary and secondary students say that they "hate" U.S. History,

English, and physics. At the collegiate level, individuals have changed majors and minors because "the field was not what they thought it would be—it was boring." Others shifted majors because of their poor scores on specific types of paper-and-pencil tests. Sadly, in all cases, there was evidence of a feeling of inadequacy.

The inability to differentiate among goals, media, and content can have devastating results. A person may think he is a failure when the problem may really lie in the methodology of teaching. Society certainly loses when a person with potential to contribute transfers from a learning area that he prefers to something that is merely more amenable.

MISMATCH IN TEACHERS

We are finding that mismatch also has an effect upon the teacher. Teachers whose teaching styles closely approximate their *major learning preferences* report comfort, ease, and authenticity. Those who venture into minor areas indicate ranges of ease through mild discomfort. Those who consistently instruct via minor styles report feelings of awkwardness, lack of efficiency and authenticity, and pain—mental and physical.

Why do some teachers chronically mismatch their learning and teaching styles? A prime reason is that they are not aware of mind-quality and stylistic differences. Pain and fatigue are viewed as natural concomitants of hard work and study—not as possible indicators of dis-ease. A second reason pertains to the perception people attach to the role label, "teacher." Many carry a distinct image of what a teacher is and accept the self-imposed image, even if it causes them pain.

A final reason arises from the willingness of many teachers to go along with traditional or required practices within a particular subject area or within a specific school. There are teachers, for example, who tell us that "poetry *must* be taught this way," and that "we can't individualize and still meet mandated behavioral objectives," or that "students are not permitted to move around my room." There is only one kind of teacher behavior in their schools.

Does self-imposed or environmentally induced mismatch result in problems for teachers? The answer is mixed. As a general rule, we have found that periodic mismatch of major preferences can be tolerated and even viewed as acceptable, as varietal, as challenging. On the other hand, prolonged and chronic mismatch can result in stress, even burnout. M. Feldenkrais saw this potential outcome: "Force that is not converted into movement does not simply disappear, but is dissipated into damage done to joints, muscles, and other sections of the body."[2] It takes little imagination to understand how chronic style mismatch can lead to serious mental, emotional, or physical problems for *both* learners and teachers.

IMPLICATIONS

Given the importance of acknowledging styles and the results of match and mismatch, what should be done? First and foremost, educators must be willing to confront the counseling and instructional implications of learning and teaching style and the problems associated with mind-quality energy flow and blockage. Along with this greater awareness, there must be more openness toward a diagnostic/prescriptive approach to instruction. For many educators, student advisement serves only a ritualistic function. Advisement meets the requirements of a law, serves a psychological need of expressing concern, addresses apparent needs of the people involved, summarizes knowledge to date, gives direction for future work. It may even minimize the need for future person-to-person encounters. All these elements can be very positive, except the last. If conferencing is assumed to be the *end*—"I have given him his annual diagnostic/prescriptive opportunity this year"—the ritual is self-deceptive for both teacher and learner. The learner is deluded into thinking that everything possible has been done for him and that subsequent problems are his own fault, not the teacher's.

To obviate this insidious situation, follow-up on diagnosis and prescription is critical. Of equal importance, *learners must be taught the language of diagnosis and prescription* so that they can participate intelligently before, during, and following the ritual. In this way they will become less dependent and more responsible for their own learning.

SUMMARY

To date, inquiries into the nature and anatomy of learning and teaching styles have lead to the following:

- Learning style consists of behaviors which give clues as to the mind-qualities an individual uses to interact with his environment and to gather and process data from it.

2. Feldenkrais, M., *Awareness Through Movement,* New York: Harper and Row, 1972, p. 58.

- Mind-qualities appear as dualities like abstract/concrete perception and inductive/deductive processing. These dualities are within us all, but they vary in inherent strength and orientation.

- Environments make adaptive demands upon individual mind-qualities.

- Learners need to recognize their inherent mediation abilities and the demands being placed upon them. They also need to learn how to add "unnatural" behaviors, to adapt, cope with, and change themselves and their environment.

- Teaching style consists of the teacher's personal behaviors and media technologies chosen to deliver and receive information.

- Energies of a teacher appear to flow easiest when his natural learning style and teaching style are parallel (matched); e.g., when as a highly deductive-oriented learner, he is able to teach in a highly deductive manner using deductive-based materials.

- Prolonged periods of matched styles can result in a comfortable "path of least resistance." Too much matching can change this path into a rut and lead to boredom.

- Energies of a teacher flow with varying degrees of difficulty and frustration when his personal learning style and teaching style are mismatched; e.g., as a highly deductive-oriented learner he finds that he must teach an extended inquiry-based lesson.

- Periods of mismatch can result in new or varied experiences, the development of new techniques, and an appreciation of how the "other half" lives. On the other hand, great mismatch can lead to frustration, anger, avoidance behaviors, and procrastination.

- Chronic periods of acute mismatch can result in major mental, emotional, and physical problems if the mismatch is not recognized and dealt with appropriately.

These summary statements outline the major interactions that come into play when schools attempt to deal with learning and teaching styles. They indicate the extent and implications of the relationships between each individual and his environment. Further, they suggest the necessity for self-knowledge, balance, alignment, and "stretching." The time has come for our schools to teach more than subject matter. It is time for them to accept the challenges of individual differences and to face squarely the need to help the teacher and the learner understand how and why human beings learn.

Chapter 3

Learning Style and Student Needs: An Introduction to Conceptual Level

David E. Hunt

Like individual differences among students, the possible variations in learning style are infinite. Described here is one learning style characteristic—need for structure—which is derived from a theoretical construct, Conceptual Level (Hunt, 1971; Hunt & Sullivan, 1974, Hunt, 1978). This single characteristic is used to illustrate: (1) how a theoretical idea can be translated into practice and (2) how learning style can serve to guide the matching of educational approaches to student needs for both facilitating learning and enhancing development.

WHAT IS LEARNING STYLE?

Good teachers have always known that students differ in how they learn. Some students learn better by listening to the teacher, some by discussion, others by working on their own, etc. Learning style, therefore, describes a student in terms of those educational conditions under which he is most likely to learn. Learning style describes *how* a student learns, not what he has learned. To say that a student differs in learning style means that certain educational approaches are more effective than others for him.

There are many different ways to consider learning style; here learning style is described in terms of how much *structure* the student requires in order to learn best. Consider a horizontal line on which educational environments, or teaching methods, are arranged in terms of their degree of structure. On the left-hand or structured side would be placed those approaches in which instructions were given clearly, the teacher explained the material, requirements were very specific, etc. On the right-hand or less structured side of the dimension would be approaches in which the student was responsible for organizing

27

his assignments, and approaches in which the teacher provided a minimum of organization.

Conceptual Level describes students in terms of their requirements for structure in an educational environment. Some students are described as needing a fairly structured environment. For example, in using a Conceptual Level paper-and-pencil test (Hunt, Butler, Noy & Rosser, 1978) with a group of Grade 6 students, the following distribution (expressed in percentages) was found. (We also include the proportions of a group of Grade 9 students to show the developmental change in learning style):

Table 1—*Need for Structure*

	Much	*Some*	*Less*
Percentage of Grade 6 students	54	31	15
Percentage of Grade 9 students	18	28	54

More than half of the Grade 6 students were in high need for structure.

The Conceptual Level matching model (Hunt, 1971) described here is based on a theory of personality development (Harvey, Hunt & Schroder, 1961). It describes students both in terms of their stage of development and their present style, so that specific matching prescriptions can be stated both for long-term and short-term purposes. For example, a student might be at a dependent, conforming stage of development (or high in his present need for structure). In dealing with such a student, a teacher would take account of his present needs to plan the short-term educational approach likely to be most effective. However, any approach should be directed to the long-term developmental goal of increasing the student's independence and initiative, i.e., extending his learning style.

How Can We View the Development of Learning Style?

The development of learning styles is considered here on a dimension of Conceptual Level (CL), or increasing self-responsibility. Although students may be described at every point on this dimension, it makes sense to summarize the developmental dimension in terms of stages, much as a motion picture sequence could be represented by selecting still shots from the sequence, as shown in Figure 1.

The sequence of stages in Figure 1 can be summarized as proceeding from an immature, unsocialized stage (A) to a dependent, conforming stage (B) to an independent, self-reliant stage (C). From a

Figure 1—*Development of Conceptual Level*

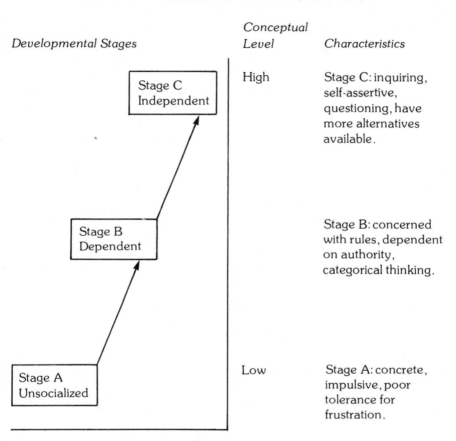

Developmental Stages

Conceptual
Level

Characteristics

Stage C
Independent

High

Stage C: inquiring,
self-assertive,
questioning, have
more alternatives
available.

Stage B
Dependent

Stage B: concerned
with rules, dependent
on authority,
categorical thinking.

Stage A
Unsocialized

Low

Stage A: concrete,
impulsive, poor
tolerance for
frustration.

developmental view, the stages can be described in terms of increasing self-responsibility, increasing understanding of oneself and others, and increasing capacity for considering alternatives. For example, a student at Stage B differs from a student at Stage C not only in his being more dependent, but also in having fewer alternatives available for considering problems.

HOW IS LEARNING STYLE ASSESSED?

Information about a student's learning style may come from many sources: the student himself, his parents, his teachers, his peers, and learning style measures. How effectively students, parents, and teachers can assess learning style depends on how well they understand the idea and how much relevant information is available. When learning style has become more familiar (and clearly distinguished from ability), it should be possible to conduct the assessment largely by students themselves, assisted by teachers and parents. Meanwhile, learning style measures provide useful information to the student, teacher, and parents to help them understand the idea.

The Paragraph Completion Method (Hunt, Butler, Noy & Rosser, 1978) has been used for the past 15 years to assess learning style as Conceptual Level. When this method is administered, a student is told that his response will give some indication about how he learns best, and that this information will be helpful in planning his educational program. The student is asked to write his response to a topic, e.g., "What I think about rules ..." in two or three sentences to describe his own feelings about the topic. He writes on six or eight topics, requiring no more than 20 minutes. (Because the method demands a certain amount of skill in writing, it has rarely been used with students below Grade 6.) Scoring is ordinarily done by a research staff member and consists of coding each response in terms of how the student processes information and how much structure he requires. Scoring is not concerned with the content, e.g., what he thinks about rules, but the *structure* of his response. His response can then be compared with those of several thousand students (in Ontario) who have completed paragraphs during the past few years. The result is a general indication of his learning style expressed in terms of how much structure he requires to learn best. This information is used as an initial guide in planning the student's educational program; it is not regarded as a static, unchanging characteristic, but as something which will develop over time. Ultimately such assessment might be carried out by the student himself with the assistance of teachers and parents.

What Is the Relation of Learning Style to Academic Ability?

A student's Conceptual Level (the degree of structure required) is relatively distinct from his ability or intelligence, and thus for students in Grade 6 and above, learning style (CL) and ability can be distinguished from one another. This is because learning style describes *how* a student learns, not how well or how much he has learned. Among students who need structure, there is a wide range of ability; indeed, there are many high ability students who require structure. It is less likely however, that there will be many low ability students who need little structure. Therefore, learning style and ability show a low, but significant relation, yet they are distinct from one another. Further, the relation decreases as students grow older. It is essential to realize that learning style is different from ability so that educational arrangements based on learning style are not confused with those based on ability. Educational procedures based on ability (e.g., streaming) are often inequitable because some students receive "more" or an "enriched" program while others do not.

CAN TEACHERS ASSESS STUDENT LEARNING STYLE?

The major difficulty with teachers' assessing learning style is in distinguishing learning style from ability. Especially in working with younger (i.e., Grade 6) students, teachers tend to equate high level verbal ability with a learning style that requires little structure. Thus, the first requirement for the teacher is to become aware of how learning style differs from ability. The second requirement is that the teacher systematically vary the structure of his approach and then observe the results. Thus, the teacher might observe students for a week in a very structured learning environment and then for a week in a very unstructured learning environment to note their different reactions and attitudes. These steps are described in the final section of this chapter.

MATCHING TO LEARNING STYLE

Matched educational environments for development, that is, those most likely to produce the stage-specific development in Figure 1, can be identified simply by asking: Given the developmental work required to progress from one stage to the next, what is the educational environment most likely to facilitate such work? For example, progression from B to C requires the student to define himself distinctively by breaking away from the general standards for everyone at Stage B.

Table 2—Matched environments for stage-specific development

Desired development	Matched environment
A → B	Highly structured, clear consistent, accepting but firm
B → C	Moderately structured, encouraging self-expression
Articulation of C	Less structured with emphasis on autonomy

Table 2 summarizes the developmental needs at each stage. It describes the general degree of structure as well as the specific nature of support required to encourage development. The stage-specific matched environments in the table should not be interpreted too literally because any development is, by definition, a long-term process over a period of years. A teacher or a parent cannot simply provide the desired environment for one day and observe developmental growth the next. Table 2, then, is not a blueprint for stimulating premature growth. Instead, it is intended to indicate those long-term environmental influences most likely to encourage development, and to put the short-term matching prescription into developmental perspective.

A student's present Conceptual Level, or position on the developmental dimension in Figure 1, can provide a current basis for matching educational approach to learning style for short-term purposes. Given the characteristics of low CL students (dependent on external standards and incapable of generating their own concepts), they should learn better with the structured approach. Given the characteristics of high CL students (capable of generating new concepts and holding internal standards), they should either learn better with low structure, or be unaffected by variations in structure, i.e. learn well in all varieties of structures. The basic CL matching principle, therefore, is: "Low CL learners profit more from high structure and high CL learners profit more from low structure, or in some cases, are less affected by variation in structure" (Hunt, 1971). Stated in this form, the principle seems obvious; certainly it is not new. Since good teachers have probably always known that students differ in how they learn, the term *learning style* is used to describe the student's CL. Learning style is defined here in terms of *how much structure* a student requires in order to learn best. Note that learning style refers to how much he *requires,* not necessarily how much he *prefers.* These relations are shown in Table 3.

Table 3—*Learning style and need for structure*

Developmental Stage	Conceptual Level	Matched Environment	Learning Style
C	High	Low structure	Need less structure
B	Low	Moderately high structure	Need some structure
A	Very low	High structure	Need much structure

The practical advantage of describing students in terms of learning style as shown in Table 3, rather than CL, is that the description is more easily translatable into how to work with a specific student. Student variation on the CL dimension can be seen as variation in terms of need for structure, as follows:

Needs much	Needs some	Needs less

<--->

DO STUDENTS HAVE THE SAME LEARNING STYLE IN DIFFERENT SUB-JECTS?

This question is complicated by the variation in the structure of the subjects themselves. Thus, mathematics is a more structured discipline than social science and, therefore, the possibility for teaching mathematics with different degrees of structure is limited by its nature. What might be an unstructured approach in mathematics might be fairly structured in social science. The difference becomes important in considering this question since what appears to be variation within a student ("Charlie works on his own in math, but needs more instruction in social science") may indicate more about the subjects than about the student. Very little research evidence is available on this question although there is a tendency for students with structured learning styles to perform better in engineering and mathematics while students who require less structure perform better in the social sciences. This difference may be due, however, to the nature of the examinations since students who require structure perform better on objective examinations while students who require less structure perform better on essay tests. It would be possible to measure a student's learning styles for each subject, but for now we continue to assess students' general learning style (primarily because teachers working with students of varying general learning style find this helpful in different subjects).

SHOULD STUDENTS BE GROUPED ACCORDING TO LEARNING STYLE?

To state that a particular student requires a certain degree of structure in his learning environment does not tell us how to provide that environment; in short, the matching principle describes what a student needs, but not precisely what educational arrangement is best suited to meet that need. Each of the educational arrangements is a way of organizing resources so that students are more likely to experience more appropriate alternatives.

Grouping students with similar learning styles is one of the most obvious methods for implementing matching ideas; this procedure has been used in several schools during the past few years. Since learning style is linked to what teaching method is used, the value of grouping is clear. However, such grouping is certainly not necessary for teaching to different learning styles. On the other hand, it does not restrict students for several reasons.

First, the students are not initially "all alike" because of their similarity in learning style; there still will be a wide variation in ability, activity, passivity, and interest, and therefore a diversity of peer stimulation available. Second, if a student's learning style in a particular subject differs from others in the group, the teacher can be more aware of this difference, and spend more time working with him than would be possible in a class of students with the entire range of learning styles. Third, as indicated, the student's present learning style can itself help define the long-term goal of growth and development.

WHAT ARE THE STEPS IN ASSESSING LEARNING STYLE?

We can describe the assessment of learning style in three steps: (1) considering degree of structure, (2) considering student characteristics, and (3) sharing impressions with other teachers when possible.

What is meant by degree of structure? Since classification on learning style involves placing a student on the "structure line," it follows that teachers need to understand something about the definition of degree of structure, i.e., how are low and high structured environments defined? The most important feature of degree of structure is how much the teacher is responsible for the learning activity (the more, the higher the structure), but variation in specificity of instructions and degree of pre-organization of material are also important. Highly structured environments are teacher-centered, include pre-organized material, and involve very specific instructions and expectations. Approaches which are low in structure are more likely to be determined by the student, involve general instructions, and include material which is not pre-organized. An understanding of the specific nature of approaches which are high or low in structure opens the possibility for the teacher to systematically vary the structure for a short time to observe how well each one has learned and how he felt. For example, a teacher might use a very structured, highly organized approach for one week and then a very unstructured approach for a second week, taking care to note student reactions to each of the two approaches. Experienced teachers have been doing this informally for years, of course, so that the only thing new about the suggestion is to be as systematic as possible both in providing *distinctively* high and low structured approaches and in observing student reactions and attitudes to each.

Characteristics of students with different learning styles. We described earlier some of the theoretically expected characteristics of students with differing needs for structure. Table 4 summarizes characteristics of students with differing learning styles as reported by their teachers. (Most of these descriptions come from junior high school

Table 4—
Characteristics of students of different learning styles

Student Learning style	Characteristics
Need very much structure	"Short attention span." "Like to be active; there is constant movement." "A lot of physical and verbal fights." "Do not know how to function in group situations or disucssion." "Incapable of thinking through a problem; will guess and let it go at that." "Try the rules often." "Work only because the teacher says and look to peers for approval."
Need much structure	"Oriented to the role of a 'good student,' one who got the right answers, had neat work and good work habits." "Seek teacher approval." "Want to work alone at their own desks." "Incapable of adjusting to a different teacher." "Upset by visitors or alterations of the schedule." "Do not express personal opinions." "Are confused by choices." "Want to be told and have the teacher constantly present."
Need less structure	"Like to discuss and argue." "Everybody wants to talk at once and nobody listens." "Will question and volunteer additional information." "Want to solve things themselves." "Go off on sidetracks." "Don't require teacher rewards." "Are imaginative." "Are not afraid of making mistakes." "Are enthusiastic and eager to go off on things on their own." "See alternatives." "Are adverse to detail and cannot tolerate going step-by-step." "May be initially self-centered and less concerned about others."

teachers working with classroom groups homogeneous in learning style.)

The characteristics in Table 4 should be thought of as guides to be used along with other information such as student response to systematic variations in degree of structure.

Classifying students and comparing classifications with others. Using what has been learned from studying specific variations in degree of structure and behavioral characteristics of various learning style groups, the teacher can classify students in terms of the "structure line." Ideally, one should rely on the observation of students under systematically varying degrees of structure, but if this is not possible, classification can be based on recalled impressions of students during the past year. In either case, wherever possible more than one teacher should be involved in the classification process, both for purposes of increasing accuracy as well as to raise issues which need further discussion.

Below are some teaching approaches that teachers have found to be successful with students of the three CL learning styles. These suggestions are geared primarily to facilitate learning rather than to encourage development.

TEACHING APPROACHES USED WITH STUDENTS WHO REQUIRE LITTLE STRUCTURE

- Allow them to select their own seats.
- Give them several topics from which to choose.
- Set weekly (or longer) assignments and allow students to make up their own timetables.
- Encourage them to use each other as resources.
- Allow more mobility and give them more opportunities to take part in planning and decision making. "If they are given the freedom to pursue things on their own, they will continue on their own without question."
- Have them work in groups with the teacher serving as a resource person.
- Approach material at a more abstract or general level. "You can start out with a discussion and then go to the facts of the material."
- Train them to listen to instructions (and to listen in general) as they tend to go off on their own.

- Remind and encourage them to take an interest in others.

TEACHING APPROACHES USED WITH STUDENTS WHO REQUIRE SOME STRUCTURE

- Arrange students initially in rows and gradually get them working in pairs, then in small groups.
- Have definite and consistent rules—let them know what is expected of them.
- Use creative drama to encourage spontaneity, self-awareness and cooperation.
- Help them to know what to do each day. Some teachers found that initialing the students' work daily provided the teacher contact they desired and the impetus to continue. They could see how much they had accomplished.
- Provide non-threatening situations where they have to risk an opinion.
- Provide a lot of praise and success-oriented situations.
- Give them group problems to encourage sharing.
- Provide opportunities for choice and decision making as they appear ready for them. Push them gently into situations where they have to make decisions and take responsibility.

TEACHING APPROACHES USED WITH STUDENTS WHO REQUIRE MUCH STRUCTURE

- Have definite and consistent rules—let them know what is expected of them.
- Give specific guidelines and instructions (step-by-step), even make a chart of the steps.
- Make goals and deadlines short and definite ("Give them the topic, how many lines/pages, how it is to be done, and the exact date it is due.")
- Provide a variety of activities during the period, incorporating some physical movement whenever possible.
- Make positive comments about their attempts; give immediate feedback on each step; give much assurance and attention; praise often.
- Use pictures and things they can see, feel and touch.

- Get them to work immediately and change the pace often.
- Display their work; it's a form of reinforcement which they like.
- Capitalize on their interests to assist them in learning the various reading skills, i.e., stories or projects dealing with cars with Grade 9 boys.
- Begin with factual material before attempting discussion.
- Move gradually from seat work to discussion; provide more group work as they are able to handle it.
- Leave them at the end of each period with the satisfaction of having learned new material and having success in what they have been studying—almost a complete lesson each period with a minor carryover to the next period and the mention of something interesting to come.
- Read to them; it helps extend their attention span and enhance listening skills.
- Give short quizzes and objective tests initially.
- Provide opportunities for choice and decision making as they appear ready for them.

A Final Comment

Learning style as Conceptual Level is only one of the infinite variations in student learning style. It can serve to guide educational approaches matched to facilitate learning as well as enhance development. Learning style as Conceptual Level is both a contemporary characteristic and an objective for development. Effective teaching requires that teachers continually "read" (assess) and "flex" (adapt) to students (Hunt, 1976). Matching to Conceptual Level provides a metaphor or guide which can sensitize teachers so that they will be able to "read" and "flex" to other learning styles in addition to Conceptual Level.

Chapter 4

Identifying Individual Learning Styles

Rita Dunn
Kenneth Dunn
Gary E. Price

We became involved with the phenomenon called "learning style" as an outgrowth of trying to help slow achieving youngsters narrow the gap between their ability to read and the grade level expectations held for them.

In 1967, the New York State Education Department asked Rita Dunn to direct The Teacher Reserve, a graduate program designed to develop teachers who were capable of helping "educationally disadvantaged" students to learn. "Mature" persons who had earned baccalaureate degrees in liberal arts areas and, therefore, had not been exposed to "traditional" classroom methodology, were recruited into a master's degree program to develop innovative instructional strategies during daytime hours and essentially in public school classrooms.

Over a three-year period, approximately 600 teachers-in-training, eight college professors, more than 20 classroom teachers, and at least five public school administrators worked together to facilitate learning for students who had not responded well to traditional teaching. Individualization was in its early stages at that time and various kinds of Learning Activity Packages (LAPS), programmed learning, and games were used and evaluated.

What became apparent was that selected methods appeared to be extremely effective with some youngsters but failed to produce anything other than minor gains with others. For example, when we used small-group techniques, certain children thrived while others avoided all peer-oriented studies. When using programmed learning, some youngsters tired easily and could not "sit still" while others would continue using the materials for hours, evidencing neither restlessness nor fatigue. Games also were intriguing to many and boring to others. Some learned rapidly with one technique; others literally despised that method and refused to be enticed into using it after initial experiences. It rapidly became evident that, if we were to help students to become academically successful, we had to develop *different* methods, and then, in some way, determine which might appeal to and be effective with selected learners.

At that time, the profession was focusing on "relevance" and its relationship to academic achievement. In one school we interviewed every student, at least one parent of each, and every teacher to identify:

- Those topics that might be interesting or relevant to students in each class;

- Those topics that each student's parent(s) believed their youngster would find interesting; and

- Those topics that each student's teacher believed would be interesting to their classes based on expressed concerns, experiences, or talents.

The findings revealed that of the three most relevant items indicated by the students, the teachers selected only one and the parents were incorrect on all three.

Using the three identified topics as the focus for our "relevant" studies (through which we planned to increase the students' reading levels), we designed Contract Activity Packages, mini-programmed learning sequences, stories and games. Again, *regardless of the curriculum*, it appeared to be the *methods* that were attracting youngsters. Furthermore, although a few students preferred alternative methods at different times or on different days, most elected to use specific methods repeatedly once they had experienced success with them. The variety of responses to different methods caused us to examine the learner more closely.

We then investigated the research within and outside the field of education concerned with how youngsters and adults learn and were amazed to find a body of knowledge that had been accumulated over an 80-year period repeatedly verifying that students acquire information and skills in many different ways (Dunn and Dunn, 1975). The educational literature yielded 18 categories that, when classified, suggested that learners are affected by: (a) the *immediate environment*, (b) *their own emotionality*, (c) *their sociological needs*, and (d) *their physical requirements*. (See Table 1) Psychological research proposed impressive evidence for a fifth dimension, cognitive style. We have more to say on that later.

We found that learning style is the manner in which at least 18 different elements from four basic stimuli affect a person's ability to absorb and retain. The combination and variations among these elements suggest that few people learn in exactly the same way, just as few people think exactly alike.

Analyzing the Basic Elements of Learning Style

Before a school staff begins to diagnose students to identify how each one learns, teachers, counselors and psychologists should understand the definitions and implications of each element that may affect people of any age.

THE ENVIRONMENTAL ELEMENTS OF LEARNING STYLE

Sound in the Environment. Some proponents of "open education" programs suggest that youngsters can work easily with noise; that they can "block out" sound or ignore it. Not so. *Some* can block out sound, and so can *some* grownups. *Some* students only need a *relatively* quiet environment while others require complete silence before they can concentrate.

There is another group of youngsters who *cannot* learn in silence. Whenever total silence is imposed on these students, they become aware of all the sounds they "never heard before." They tend to reach out and turn on music whenever they begin to study; the melodies (rock or other) block out the extraneous sounds that might otherwise interrupt their trains of thought. Even television is used by some as a combination security blanket and sound screen.

These characteristics are identifiable in some students of all ages. Some can function in one way, others in the exact opposite mode. Knowing this, we can understand how necessary it is to design an instructional environment that includes areas where students that "need to" may talk, interact, and share, and areas where others may work alone in quiet. Both types of youngsters may be found in any randomly selected group. We must also remember that sound (or its absence) is not a factor for some students.

Light in the Environment. Light is a factor that appears to affect fewer people than does sound. Although some students are light-sensitive and can tolerate only subdued lighting, and others are light-needy and require extremely bright lights before they can comfortably engage in reading or writing activities, most seem to be relatively unaffected by normal variations of light.

However, when pilot-testing our original learning style question-

Table 1

ELEMENTS

STIMULI				
ENVIRONMENTAL	SOUND	LIGHT	TEMPERATURE	DESIGN
EMOTIONAL	MOTIVATION	PERSISTENCE	RESPONSIBILITY	STRUCTURE
SOCIOLOGICAL	COLLEAGUES / SELF	PAIR	TEAM	AUTHORITY / VARIED
PHYSICAL	PERCEPTUAL	INTAKE	TIME	MOBILITY
PSYCHOLOGICAL	ANALYTIC / GLOBAL $\frac{6}{-3}$	FIELD INDEPENDENT / FIELD DEPENDENT		REFLECTIVE / IMPULSIVE

naire, we found one or two youngsters in almost every group who in-tensely disliked camera bulb flashes, sitting near brightly lit windows, or the glare on beaches. It was also true that many students appeared to be oblivious to light unless the environment changed and became "dark" to them; at that point, they missed the light that they were unaware of previously.

Youngsters who tend to prefer subdued light often recount their parents' repeated cautions against reading "in the dark," and yet they rarely remembered to turn on the additional lights that the adults thought necessary. The likely reason is that they feel comfortable with-out them. These learners report that they grow tense when the light-ing becomes excessive for them.

People who require a brightly lighted environment describe the reverse reaction. If the lighting is inadequate, they tend to become apathetic and find it difficult to remain alert. For them, bright light serves as an energizer.

Temperature in the Environment. Many of us have had the exper-ience of being in either a room or car feeling cold and requesting that the air-conditioning be lowered, only to be derided because others felt warm. Or, we have had the reverse happen—feeling uncomfort-ably hot while others complained of being cool. We can also remem-ber when, as children, we were admonished to wear sweaters or other garments when going outdoors and felt "put upon" because we were warm and did not feel that we needed the additional clothing.

One of the more humorous incidents that occurred when we were testing students centered around a class discussion of definitions. When asked to explain the word "sweater," one bright boy answered, "A sweater is something my mother makes me wear when *she* is cold!"

Individual reactions to temperature are unique. Some men and women can concentrate better when the environment is cool (or cold); when it becomes "warm," they feel drowsy and cannot function well. Others cannot concentrate when they are cool; anything other than warmth (and what is "warm" to one is not to another) can cause physical and/or emotional discomfort which reduces productivity.

Since differences in tolerance to temperature vary, how can we determine what might be the "best" thermometer setting for each classroom? Obviously, we can't for there is no "best" setting. We need to be aware of which sections of each room provide the most and the least warmth at various times of the year, and then permit students whose learning style requirements are fostered by being either near or away from those sections, to *choose* where they will work and learn.

If you are beginning to question how one small classroom that seems crowded *now* can incorporate enough areas to accommodate students who need verbal interaction, silence, soft music to block out sound, intense light, subdued light, coolness, and warmth, do not be concerned. When people say, "It can't be done!" they are merely articulating that *they* don't know how to do it. There are many low cost ways of redesigning ordinary classrooms to provide for students with varied learning styles (Dunn and Dunn, 1978).

Design in the Environment. When you read or write something that requires effort, do you find that you invariably migrate toward an easy chair, a lounge, a bed, or carpeting? If that is your usual way of concentrating on a task, you may be a person who requires an "informal" design, one that is relaxed and casual.

Conversely, you may not be able to study in informal facilities; these may *prevent* you from producing or may make you drowsy and unable to achieve. Some people must actually sit on a hard chair at a library-type table in order to concentrate. For others, highly formal physical surroundings suppress motivation and creativity. There are some people, of course, for whom design is no problem, or for whom design needs vary with the type of motivation they feel toward the task.

Let's translate a need for either a formal or an informal study design to the classroom. Youngsters who think best when relaxed, who often do their homework on the floor or in an easy chair, may find it difficult to be seated (particularly for long periods of time) at a desk. Students rarely conform to standard sizes and shapes; many are bigger than the uniform seats provided and, after a short interval, begin to squirm in discomfort. Teachers may not understand that young, growing bodies used to continual activity find it difficult to be passive in situations that require conformity and longevity. This lack of understanding can lead to friction between the teacher and the youngster, yet could easily be reduced, if not eliminated, if the student were permitted to work quietly in an informal area of the room. It really shouldn't matter *where* the youngster learns, as long as he does learn.

THE EMOTIONAL ELEMENTS OF LEARNING STYLE

Motivation as a Function of Emotion. Most of us acknowledge that teachers should not teach motivated and unmotivated students in the same way; yet often they do exactly that, with predictable consequences for erupting discipline problems and student and teacher dissatisfaction. Motivated youngsters are eager to learn; they should be told exactly what they are required to do, which resources are available to them, how to get help if they should need it, and how they will be expected to demonstrate what they have been assigned to learn.

Unmotivated students should be given very *short* assignments. They must be given resources that complement their perceptual strengths. If they learn more easily by hearing, rather than by reading, they should be given the appropriate book (s) and a cassette tape recording of someone reading that section of the book which responds to the assignment. It is possible to have a capable student or parent read small sections of a required text onto a tape or cassette for repeated use by poor readers.

Furthermore, since many poorly motivated students are unenthusiastic about learning because they find it so difficult to achieve, the use of programmed learning, contracts, or multisensory instructional packages as substitutes for class lectures or discussion may help them learn and develop a better self image. A student who is not motivated in a fairly conventional setting may become extremely interested in achieving in an individualized program. Such youngsters may be able to function responsibly when given opportunities to make choices, to learn in accordance with their learning style preferences, to participate in paired or teamed peer group studies, and to self- or peer test to evaluate themselves.

Persistence as a Function of Emotion. When given a task to perform, some students will work at it until it has been completed. If they develop a problem with the assignment, they will find a classmate or a resource reference to explain how to overcome the difficulty. If no other help is available, they will seek the teacher's assistance and then return to their work.

Other students, often those we say have "short attention spans," cannot continue their work for any length of time. The moment these youngsters experience any difficulty, they lose interest, become irritated, begin to daydream, and/or become involved in social activities rather than complete their tasks. Just as students in a given group should be assigned different objectives based partially on their ability levels and interests, so should the length and type of assignment be varied based on the teacher's observations of student ability to "stay with" a task. Students who find it difficult to sustain attention for 20 to 30 minutes will bear a double burden—the learning itself and learning within a time span that taxes their emotions and ability to function without becoming disruptive. This is one example where "self-pacing" should be considered.

Students should be given learning objectives and a time interval in which to complete them, with a clear understanding that although they need not work continuously, they must complete the learning tasks. Students who need frequent relaxation periods may be emotionally able to acquire the prescribed knowledge and skills in their own way—in a flexible time period and in accordance with their total learning style.

This is an area in which the teacher will need to experiment. Some students will require a few simple tasks of relatively short duration to function adequately on an independent basis; others will be able to cope with longer tasks of varied complexity. An observation period in which students begin with a few objectives and proceed toward tasks of increasing complexity and duration may be the most effective way of assessing a student's persistence quotient.

Responsibility as a Function of Emotion. Every teacher recognizes and appreciates responsible students. Invariably, these youngsters follow through on a given task, complete it to the best of their ability, and often do so without direct or frequent supervision. They only require:

- Clearly stated assignments that can be understood and completed,
- Resources that provide information on a level with which they can cope,
- An indication of where assistance may be obtained if the task becomes difficult,
- Suggestions for testing themselves to determine progress and any aspects that require further study, and
- Alternative ways to demonstrate their achievement of the objectives.

Unfortunately, many students are not responsible. When a task becomes difficult for them, rather than seek help, they permit their attention to wander. Sometimes they begin to annoy their classmates, become troublesome and cause a general disturbance. It is necessary to use methods with these young people that are different from those suggested for responsible youngsters.

When students cannot learn easily, they are likely to become discouraged or irritated. To help students to avoid such self-defeating reactions, it is necessary to test them in order to identify the way(s) in which they are most likely to achieve. Then the method(s) that respond most closely to their learning style characteristics should be introduced.

For example, a slow learning student who does not read well should be given short assignments, written materials that are also available on a supplementary tape, and much supervision, encouragement and praise as each objective is completed. For youngsters who do not understand what they are reading, either an accompanying tape to explain the written content or tactual kinesthetic "games" should be available. For students who cannot learn alone, use small group techniques. For those who need structure and cannot work with peers, use programmed learning. For those who are slow learners, use multi-sensory instructional packages (Dunn and Dunn, 1978).

As students begin to achieve and feel increased confidence, their assignments may be lengthened or made slightly more demanding. Expect that individuals will *behave* responsibly when they are able to do what is required without fear of either embarrassment or failure. Teachers should provide support and not demand more than the student can achieve; many *become* "irresponsible" when they realize that their serious efforts cannot produce success.

Structure as a Function of Emotion. Structure is the establishment of specific rules for working on and completing an assignment. It implies that certain things should be completed in a special way within a definite time span. Structure limits the number of options that are available to a student and imposes modes of learning, responding, or demonstrating achievement.

Although creative youngsters squirm under strict guidelines and find learning that way frustrating and unstimulating, others find it equally difficult to achieve *without* an imposed structure. It is necessary, therefore, to identify creative learners who would thrive when offered varied opportunities to organize their own studying situations. It is equally important to recognize those who are unable to function comfortably unless well-defined directions and procedures are given to them.

Consider, for example, the teacher who asks an entire class to write a composition about "something that interests you." The creative, experienced, or alert student may consider many possible themes, and may not be able to choose one from among the many that come to mind. Less creative students and those with learning disabilities may not be able to identify a single idea to describe. In both cases, some structure is needed. For those who think of many ideas, a limit of subject, time or acceptable alternatives might be appropriate. For those who cannot think of anything, the teacher might offer some possibilities and suggest that they select one from among those listed. A few others may need counseling and direction to settle on any topic.

Motivated, persistent, responsible students usually require little structure and supervision, certainly far less than do the unmotivated, the impersistent, and the irresponsible. The creative youngster who can make decisions usually requires very little structure. As teachers observe students in a learning situation, they begin to recognize who needs more or less well-defined guidelines and who responds better to options and choices while learning.

The Sociological Elements of Learning Style. For years teachers directly "taught" their students whatever had to be learned. When youngsters had difficulty in acquiring knowledge, teachers believed that their charges had not "paid attention." Few realized that, despite the quality of the teaching, some students are incapable of learning from an adult. These young people are uncomfortable when under pressure to concentrate, whether it be a teacher or other "authority" figure. They are fearful of failing, embarrassed to show inability, and, as a result, often become too tense to concentrate. For these students, either learning alone or with peers is a better alternative than working directly in a pressure situation with their teachers.

Conversely, despite the recently coined generalization that "young people learn better from other young people than they do from their teachers," some students are unable to study or concentrate when involved with their peers. Rather than learn, they socialize. In other instances, certain youngsters are ashamed to let their friends or classmates see that they cannot learn easily; and rather than admit their discomfort, they pretend to dislike their studies. In either case, this type of student may *need* an adult teacher in order to achieve. Those who cannot learn from peers often resent being required to do so and, of course, some students have little desire to teach others.

Contrary to widespread belief, there is no single way to group students for maximum learning. Students can learn in a variety of sociological patterns that include working alone, with one or two friends, in a small group or as part of a team, with adults, or some variation of these. It is important to identify how each student learns and then to assign to that individual the correct grouping, method(s), and resources.

How a student learns socially is easily recognized when youngsters are permitted to select the ways they will complete their assignments. Some learners will elect to work with friends, of course, and rather than study together, they will socialize and, in a sense, prevent each other from achieving. In these cases, the teacher needs to intervene. Unless the pair (group, team) approaches learning soberly and can evidence achievement, members should be reassigned and prevented from working together. When a warning fails, and the students do not demonstrate sufficient growth toward completion of their objectives, the grouping should be dispersed.

THE PHYSICAL ELEMENTS OF LEARNING STYLE

Perceptual Strengths as an Element of Physical Needs. Ask almost any educator whether people learn through different senses, and the response is bound to be "yes." That knowledge, however, is rarely translated into classroom practice. It has been estimated that 90 percent of all instruction occurs through the "lecture and/or the "question and answer" methods, and yet, *only between two and three students in each group of 10 learn best by listening.*

Years ago the research data tended to be confusing because studies most frequently concerned only listening and seeing. Since a choice between the two senses was the *only* choice, findings tended to verify that either one or the other was superior. Prior to the 1960s, researchers did not examine individual youngsters to identify whether *each* learned better or less well through methods and/or materials that emphasized either their auditory or visual perceptions. Nor were investigators aware that some people learn by touching (tactile) and others by experiential or whole body (kinesthetic) instruction. Indeed, some youngsters learn best through a combination of two or more senses.

Most schools operate as if all students were able to learn to read through *any* method—whichever system the teacher is familiar with is the one that is used to teach the children in that class. This fallacious reasoning is based on a lack of understanding of individual differences.

- Youngsters who learn through their *auditory* sense can differentiate among sounds and can reproduce symbols, letters, or words by "hearing" them. These students should be taught to read through a *phonics* approach.

- Youngsters who learn through their *visual* sense can associate shapes and words and conjure up the image of a form by "seeing" it in their mind's eye. These students can learn through a *word-recognition* approach.

- Youngsters who learn through their *tactual* sense cannot begin to associate word formations and meanings without involving the sense of touch. These students should be given many experiences: (1) tracing words in sand, salt, or on clay; (2) writing the words on a chalkboard with water or chalk and on paper with pencils, crayons, and a pen; and (3) piecing together the words with sandpaper letters (picked up without looking-just by feeling-from among many such alphabetical forms in a shoebox or other container), or letter forms made of felt, nylon, burlap, etc.

- Youngsters who learn through their *kinesthetic* sense need to have "real-life" experiences in order to learn to recognize words and their meanings. Examples of activities that provide for the "whole-body" involvement of these students would include the teaching of new words by baking or cooking and focusing on the words in the recipe, including the words in directions for building something, or taking a trip and using the new vocabulary as part of the planning, the implementation, and the review.

- Youngsters who require a *combination* of senses should be taught through multisensory resources. For example, the text of a book should be read onto a cassette, and students encouraged to follow the print as the tape "speaks." Learners who are not auditory may need a combination of visual and tactual or tactual and kinesthetic resources. For these students it is wise to attach either a tactual or kinesthetic game (depending upon the student's stronger perceptual sense) to the reading materials.

- Youngsters with learning disabilities or those who do not learn easily should also be provided multi-sensory materials. Instructional packages that combine auditory, visual, tactual, and kinesthetic activities to teach a single concept or skill would be the most effective way to introduce reading to these students.

Intake as an Element of Physical Need. Observe children as they study or adults as they focus on a task that requires continued concentration. Many take periodic "breaks" and make a beeline for the refrigerator. Some nibble; others drink. Some may smoke or chew gum. This need for intake, although affecting only a part of the population, is nevertheless evidenced by many learners.

Physicians suggest that food is often sought to replace the energy being expended; or simply to relax the tension that some people experience when concentrating. Whatever the reason, we have found that when some youngsters are permitted to eat while they are learning, their grades *and* their attitudes improve.

Keep an *eye* out for the student who, while concentrating, bites on nails, pencils or other objects. A longing for intake rather than nerves may be prompting the action.

Time as an Element of Physical Need. The proverbial night owl and early risers are diametrically opposite in their learning styles; one comes alive late at night, and the other functions at maximum capacity early in the morning. This is true of students at all ages. Some people can perform well at one time of day, and others achieve most effectively at the extreme opposite time. Ask yourself whether you fall into the group that functions best either early in the morning or late at night? Are you a mid-morning bright star? Is it after lunch that your head appears to be clearest? Or is it late in the afternoon that things of concern come best into focus for you?

Years ago, education professors told their students, "Teach reading and math early in the morning, for that's when students are most alert." Nonsense! Some youngsters perform at maximum capacity very early in the morning while others really do not seem to awaken until late morning or noon; their most efficient functioning may vary from early morning to late at night. Can the instructional environment be arranged to permit such a wide diversity of time functioning? Absolutely, particularly with junior and senior high school students where an open campus approach is possible or an independent study program may allow for instructional packages to be taken home and studied in the evening.

Mobility as an Element of Physical Need. Frequently those youngsters who receive the most discipline are the ones who are the least capable of reacting positively to it. Teachers assume that restless students require regimentation. They do not realize that some students need a great deal of mobility in the learning environment and cannot function well unless permitted to vary their stance, posture, and location. Other youngsters are able to complete a task while maintaining one physical position for a comparatively long period of time. The desire for mobility is a conglomerate function of one's physical, emotional, and environmental reactions; but most students cannot easily control their need to move while learning.

Students who require extensive mobility should be assigned to an informal setting where their frequent changes of position will not interfere with either the way the teacher is teaching or the style of other learners. Programs that respond to the mobility needs of youngsters are usually "individualized" or "open" (Dunn and Dunn, 1974). In any event, it is important to "schedule" mobility for those who require it. Short assignments at different locations will aid these students to learn more effectively.

Developing an Instrument To
Diagnose Learning Style

In 1968-69 we developed and experimented with the first series of questions designed to elicit student predispositions toward specific learning style elements. Several research studies have demonstrated that (1) students *can* identify their own learning styles; (2) when exposed to a teaching style consonant with the ways they believe they learn, students *score higher* on tests and factual knowledge, have better attitudes, and are more efficient than when taught in a manner that is dissonant with their learning style; and (3) it is advantageous to *teach and test* students in their preferred modalities. (Domino, 1970, and Farr, 1971)

During the following five years, we continuously tested and revised the developing instrument, often with the help of graduate students at St. John's University, seven school districts in Nassau County, New York, and the Board of Cooperative Educational Services (BOCES) in that county. By 1974, reliability and consensual validity had been established and much empirical data had been accumulated.

In 1974, Gary Price conducted a content analysis of each of the questionnaire items and isolated those that achieved 90 percent consistency or better. A shortened form, the Learning Style Inventory (LSI) was developed. Reliability and face, construct, and predictive validity were assessed. During the past few years, continuing research with students in many school districts has verified the individuality of how youngsters tend to function and learn.

In the LSI, students answer a series of questions concerned with their environmental, emotional, sociological, and physical preferences and the way(s) in which they believe they behave in certain situations. Their responses are fed into a computer system which yields an itemization of those learning style elements that are important for each individual student. A manual provides guidelines for the kind of prescriptions that probably would be effective for that youngster. Alternatives are suggested if the specific element indicates more than one resource or method. When a group (or class) of students is tested simultaneously, the teacher also is provided with the number of students who indicate identical learning style characteristics. With this information, the teacher becomes aware of the number of resources of each type that will be needed and the size of the instructional area that will be necessary for those who should be working in silence, with a peer or two, with the teacher, etc. The teacher is able to design an optimum learning environment for individuals and groups with similar learning patterns.

Implications of Learning Style Data

Continuing studies with the LSI have uncovered information which had not been available previously. For example, it is possible to predict which students will function well in a traditional, an individualized, an open or an alternative program based on the data yielded through the LSI computer program (Dunn and Dunn, 1974; Martin, 1977). It is also possible to determine which resources (programs, tapes, instructional packages or contracts, films, games or small group techniques) will assist individual students to achieve. Other studies of the perceptual strengths of individuals yielded essentially similar insights (Reinert, 1976).

Studies with teachers in New York State suggest that, without training, they are able to identify only a few learning style characteristics (Dunn, Dunn and Price, 1977 and Marcus, 1977); with background and the LSI, their ability to diagnose and prescribe accurately increases substantially.

Moreover, we are finding that the majority of the students tested are *not* auditory learners, results which certainly do not support the widespread use of the "lecture" method. It appears that many students are tactual (the need to learn through touching) and/or kinesthetic (whole body, "doing," or experiencing) learners. The tendency to learn through the latter two senses appears to decrease with maturity, but at least one third of each high school sample tested exhibited such predispositions. Research also indicates that some students have strong perceptual strengths in several areas and that, almost without exception, these prove to be the high achievers. Slower learners tend to be either essentially tactual, visual-tactual, or tactual-kinesthetic — ways in which the majority of instruction does *not* occur for poor or nonreaders at the high school level. Another interesting finding is that kinesthetic learners appear to be in need of frequent mobility; they find it difficult to "sit" and, of course, to "listen" for substantial amounts of time.

ADDITIONAL EMERGING ELEMENTS OF LEARNING STYLE

"Cognitive style" appears to be still another dimension of the learning process. Although the terms cognitive and learning style often are used interchangeably in the literature, they are different but complementary. As indicated previously, learning style is the way in which individuals respond to *environmental, emotional, sociological,* and *physical* stimuli, whereas cognitive style suggests ways in which responses are made because of individual *psychological* differences. Indeed, cognitive style may be one subcategory of learning style —the psychological component.

Some of the elements of cognitive style consider whether a person is: field dependent or independent (Witkin, 1954; Kagan and Wright, 1963; Hunt, 1972); global or analytic (Thornell, 1977; Coop and Sigel, 1971; Ogunyemi, 1973); concrete, abstract, random or sequential (Gregorc, 1977); risk-taking or cautious (Kagan, 1971); responsive to hemispheric dominance (Chall and Mersky, 1978; Zenhausern, 1978); representative of selected symbolic orientations, cultural determinants, and/or modalities of inference (Hill, 1976); or reflective or impulsive (Weisberger, 1971).

Overlap appears to occur among various elements of cognitive style and between them and selected elements of learning style. For example, field dependence/independence, locus of control (whether a person is "internally" or "externally" motivated), and a person's sociological orientation (self, peer, adult, authoritarian) all suggest commonalities. Similarly, whether a person is reflective or impulsive appears to be related to whether he/she is cautious or risk-taking, and also may be related to a need for either structure or options. Furthermore, global behaviors appear to parallel field dependent manifestations, just as analytic styles seem to be field independent and, in some respects, both may be related to sociological needs. Because of the suggested interrelationships among these various elements, cognitive style deserves to be incorporated into our larger learning style model —regardless of the fact that extensive field studies must be undertaken before we can develop a precise understanding of how cognitive style of learning affects schooling.

Conclusion

The education profession is on the threshold of an instructional revolution that promises improved learning opportunities for many youngsters who heretofore have been unable to achieve well in traditional secondary schools. For example, at least two studies have demonstrated that matching instruction to individual's styles produces significant academic gain (Martin, 1977; Trautman, 1979). This implies that, prior to assigning students to either a specific program, a teaching style, or a set of resources, a school should diagnose students' learning styles and determine, in advance, their likelihood of success in a given learning situation. Indeed, all students should be placed in programs that enhance their most effective learning style.

Chapter 5

A Brain-Behavior Analysis of Learning Styles

Armin P. Thies

Learning style analysis is an issue of growing importance in the educational community. Various characteristics of learning style have been identified. Those conditions that maximize a student's performance define that person's "learning style." Much research has been done and some test instrumentation has been developed in this complex field. The *Learning Styles Inventory* (LSI) by Dunn, Dunn, and Price (1975) is one such instrument to assess personal characteristics and classroom conditions affecting learning.

An examination of the content of the *LSI* reveals that the dimensions treated fall into three categories: a) the physical environment; b) the structure and organization of the curriculum and teaching methods; and c) the individual characteristics of the student. The first two categories can readily be controlled by the teacher, and the characteristics of the student are either observable or testable. The LSI is designed to yield information about a student's learning style which has direct application for instruction. The simplicity and economy of the scale is further enhanced by permitting the students to report the conditions under which they best learn.

The LSI defines learning styles in terms of conditions which the teacher can change rather than as variables which directly cause learning. For example, light is one of the environmental elements of learning styles. Although no direct connection exists between light and learning, lighting probably influences learning because of some intermediate reason like pain resulting from sensitivity or conditioned anxiety. These intermediate explanations fall into two major categories, psychological and physical.

Conditioned anxiety is an example of a psychological explanation for preferring to learn from one's peers rather than from adults. The child is anxious with adults because of previous experience. There is no intrinsic fear of peers. Physically, the elements of learning style can be said to influence learning by their impact on the functioning of the brain. The manner in which the brain functions is relatively consistent among individuals, but variations can occur as the result of inheritance or previous experience.

In this article, the elements of learning style (Dunn and Dunn, 1978) will be interpreted in terms of their impact on brain functioning, thus providing a brain-behavior model of learning styles. Presentation of this model is not meant to imply that the elements of learning style affect learning only in the manner discussed. However, a consideration of the possible neuropsychological correlates of learning style will, at least, provide a greater appreciation for the complexity that underlies one's learning style.

See Table 1 in chapter 4, page 42 for the elements of learning style as defined by Dunn and Dunn (1975, 1979). Of the five learning style elements, the sociological elements have no apparent brain-behavior component. Preference for age of instructor or type of social interaction while learning seems to be determined solely by previous experience. Therefore, only the environmental, emotional, physical, and psychological elements will be discussed.

Environmental Factors

The environmental conditions in the classroom form the background against which learning occurs. Common sense would suggest that students prefer certain sounds, light, temperature, and design because they are most "comfortable" under such conditions and better able to concentrate on the school assignment. A brain-behavior model, however, suggests that this assumption is not always true. In brain functioning, the "background" against which information is received, processed, stored, and acted upon is termed "cortical tone." The brain is always active, but more so in waking than when asleep. The reticular activating system is responsible for maintaining cortical tone.

Because anatomical relationships are important in a brain-behavior model, it is necessary to introduce and define some terms. Figure 1 presents the most common view of the brain. Convoluted grey matter forms the cerebral cortex or cerebrum. The cerebral cortex is divided into two hemispheres by a deep fissure running between them. The left hemisphere is shown in Figure 2. The lobes and other important features are labeled for reference in reading the discussion to follow.

Figure 2 shows the brain split along the fissure that divides the brain

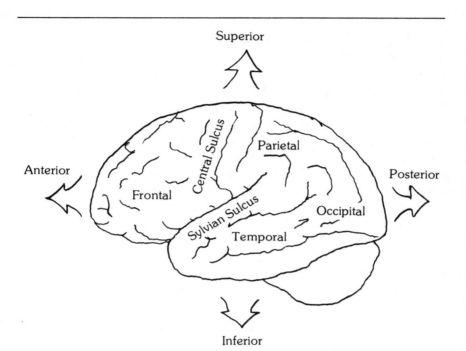

Superior

Anterior

Central Sulcus

Parietal

Frontal

Sylvian Sulcus

Occipital

Temporal

Posterior

Inferior

Figure 1. *Anatomy of the Left Hemisphere of the Brain Showing the Cerebral Lobes and Anatomical Directions*

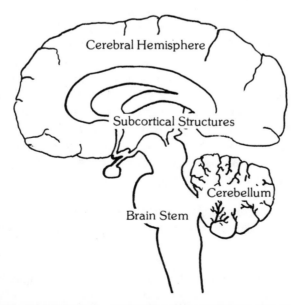

Cerebral Hemisphere

Subcortical Structures

Cerebellum

Brain Stem

Figure 2. *Medial Section of the Brain and Brain Stem*

into the right and left hemispheres, with the left hemisphere removed. Beneath the cerebral cortex there are many subcortical structures (i.e., structures below the cortex), including the brain stem which connects the brain to the spinal cord. The reticular activating system is a diffuse network of nerve cells which runs through the brain stem and has connections with the various subcortical structures and with the frontal lobes. When this system of nerve cells is stimulated, excitations spread throughout the brain, "waking" various parts in preparation for processing information. Nerves from the sense organs such as the eyes and ears on the periphery of the body run through the subcortical structures on their way to the cerebral cortex. Therefore, they can stimulate the reticular activating system which in turn prepares the brain to receive impulses from the sense organs. Learning style elements of sound, light, and temperature may have their impact on learning in this manner. The element of design, however, is more associated with the focusing of attention which is partially volitional and involves frontal lobe functioning in association with the reticular activating system.

Physical Factors

The excitation of the brain involves energy. As would be expected, the reticular activating system is also affected by metabolism. The physical element of intake may primarily affect learning through the reduction of anxiety, but the net effect of intake, especially for students who prefer to consume high energy foods such as sugar, is to increase metabolic sources of energy for brain activation. Perhaps food preferences need to be studied in this context. The physical element of time of day is also tied to metabolic cycles which vary levels of energy.

Mobility, on the other hand, may be either an attempt to increase cortical tone or a reflection of an aroused cortex. These two explanations parallel the complementary theories for organically-based hyperactivity. The "under-aroused" theories hypothesize that hyperactive children are extremely active in order to excite a chronically under-aroused nervous system. Alternatively, the "over-aroused" theories postulate that hyperactivity represents excessive reaction to stimulation by a chronically oversensitive nervous system. In either case, mobility is the result.

The simple preference for perceptual modality (the perceptual element of learning style) reflects the largest and most complex portion of cerebral functioning, equivalent to Luria's second functional unit of the brain (Luria, 1973). The temporal, parietal, and occipital lobes are each primarily concerned with the processing of information from a specific perceptual modality—visual or auditory or tactile. The temporal lobe processes auditory information. The parietal lobe processes tactile and kinesthetic information, and the occipital lobe receives visual information. Intermodality processing occurs in the area where these three lobes meet. Preference for a particular perceptual modality may reflect dysfunctioning in one or more of the lobes, subsuming the other modalities.

This picture is complicated by the *lateralization* of more complex processes. In most persons, the left hemisphere processes auditory, visual, and tactile information which is linguistic in character. The right hemisphere primarily processes visual-spatial, synthetical, and non-linguistic materials. Thus, it is possible that a child may have one perceptual preference for English and another for art.

Emotional Factors

The emotional elements of learning style contain common factors of sustained attention, organization, the structuring of work and verification of work completed. These are primarily functions of the frontal lobes. Dysfunctioning in the frontal lobes can result in extreme proneness to distraction, a disorganization of the learner's problem-solving strategies, a tendency to repeat behaviors which have already been performed, or an apparent apathy. There can be a loss of linkage between verbal awareness of an intended action and motor performance of the act. An individual may verbally report the intention to perform some action, but never complete it.

Again, the differences between the hemispheres in complex functioning also affect emotional and motivational elements of learning. Damage to the right hemisphere with its global, synthetical, simultaneous processes can result in general apathy or disregard for learning deficits. Dysfunctioning of the left hemisphere with its analytical, sequential processes may result in over-concern for the quality of performance and in excessive anxiety.

Psychological Factors

Recently the Dunns have expanded their model to include psychological elements of learning style that represent dimensions long studied and reported in the psychological literature as "cognitive styles." The first of these psychological elements is an analytic versus global dichotomy. Although the left hemisphere in most people processes linguistic material, both hemispheres are involved in complex thinking on either verbal or nonverbal tasks. The left hemisphere functioning has been described as analytic and is analogous to the analytic learning style. In the same manner, right hemisphere functioning has been described as synthetic, which is analogous to the global learning style.

Thus far only the similarity between characteristics of hemispheric functioning and the psychological learning styles has been noted. More is involved in an analytic versus global learning style, however, than the relative contribution of one side of the brain versus the other. Almost any curriculum content can be structured to facilitate analytic versus global learning as defined by available research. Some of the methods for promoting one or the other learning style do not appear, on the face of them, to promote involvement of one or the other hemisphere in the learning process.

The second psychological element is field independence versus field dependence. This dimension was originally defined by judgments of subjects based on visual and sensory perceptions while suspended in an experimental apparatus. Subsequent research found many psychological characteristics that contrasted those persons who relied on internal versus external cues to make their perceptual judgments. It would seem that any learning style which originates from such a heavily perceptual basis would reflect some processes of the nervous system. Yet if learning style is defined primarily by its psychological correlates, the connection between brain functioning and field independence versus dependence is more, not less, remote.

The final psychological element describes a reflective versus an impulsive learning style. At this time, only the impulsive end of this dimension has been demonstrated to have a neuropsychological basis—when impulsivity is extreme and neurological in nature. Impulsivity is facilitated by anxiety or chronic increases in cortical excitation resulting from disturbances of the reticular activating system or frontal lobe functioning. Many overtly "hyperactive" children may fall into this latter group.

A Partial Explanation

In conclusion, brain-behavior analysis of learning styles can only partially explain the relationships between the elements of learning style and performance in the classroom. But such explanations can further sensitize teachers to the true nature of the learning process. With increased complexity of understanding can come increased accuracy in facilitating learning. In most cases the Learning Styles Inventory appears to serve a very useful purpose by providing a relatively simple way of facilitating learning when a more detailed analysis of the child's learning is not warranted because of the expense and time required.

Chapter 6

Learning Styles of the Gifted

Shirley A. Griggs
Gary E. Price

Do gifted students show any learning style preference not shared by average junior high school students? To answer this intriguing question, the authors studied a group of 170 seventh, eighth and ninth graders from a New York City area junior high school. (This was 90 percent of the school's population.)

After gifted and average students were identified using the Lorge-Thorndike Test of Mental Ability and the Stanford Achievement Tests, all students completed the Learning Style Inventory (Dunn, Dunn & Price, 1975) to determine their learning style preferences. The LSI examines 18 style elements in four broad dimensions: environmental, emotional, sociological, and physical.

The study showed some definable differences between the gifted and the average. There were five LSI variables that differentiated significantly between gifted and non-gifted. The gifted were less teacher motivated, more persistent, liked some sound in their learning environment when studying or concentrating, did not like auditory learning, and preferred to learn alone. The non-gifted were more teacher motivated, less persistent, liked quiet when studying, preferred auditory learning, and did not want to learn alone. With these five variables alone, it was possible to predict seven out of 10 times, using discriminate analysis, which students in the group were gifted.

The elements of teacher motivated, persistence, and sound discriminated the most between the gifted and non-gifted.

These results are not surprising.

In 1965, Torrance found that gifted youth are more perseverant, self-directed, and independent than average youngsters. Steele (1971) discovered different patterns of instructional climate in studying more than 130 classes of junior and senior high school students in Illinois.

In gifted classes, there was only a moderate amount of teacher talk and real enthusiasm showed in almost all the groups. There was much opportunity for independent effort and the focus was on the student taking an active role. By comparison, average classes were more teacher dominated, the majority lacked enthusiasm and there was little opportunity for independent learning. The focus was on the teacher as information giver with a passive role for the students.

Treffinger (1967) feels that the real goal in the education of the gifted must be to cultivate self-directed learning. This goal aptly fits the characteristics of gifted youth—critical thinking ability, independence of thought and judgment, self-starting, and perserverance (Torrance, 1965). The first step toward self-directed learning is diagnosis of student characteristics, a teacher responsibility. Dunn and Dunn (1978) have determined that teachers can be trained to identify student learning preferences and to set up learning environments geared to those styles. The Dunns and Price (1977) have shown that not only do students prefer to learn in individual ways, but there is a relationship between learning and achievement in math and reading.

Goldberg (1965) suggests that the two great research needs today regarding the gifted are: "(a) the field of content and method and (b) the identification of talent among culturally and economically disadvantaged groups in our population." The first category focuses on the areas of program of study, individual student schedules and the ways in which teachers interact with students. The second raises the question of *diagnosis*—finding better ways to discover the hidden talents of students who grow up in culturally different or economically disadvantaged environments.

With the increased emphasis on the identification of the gifted student and the goal of providing differentiated educational programs to meet individual needs, it is important that educators realize that persons are different in the ways they prefer to learn. It is particularly critical that we recognize that the gifted, a unique source of talent in our population, prefer to learn in uniquely different ways as early as the junior high school age.

Chapter 7

SRI Student Perceiver Interview

Kenton R. Hill

Most of us are quite familiar with the statement attributed to Will Rogers, "I never met a man I didn't like." Perhaps we are equally familiar with the words of the boy who made his way to Boys Town, Nebraska, with his brother on his back: "He ain't heavy, he's my brother." These two statements come to mind when we consider the impact the SRI Student Perceiver Interview has had on educators—student growth facilitators—who have developed competency in the use of the process.

Teachers, counselors, psychologists, and administrators who use the SRI Student Perceiver Interview often offer comments similar to the Boys Town slogan and the Will Rogers' philosophy:

> I've never interviewed a student I didn't like. And that isn't always the case when I start the interview.

> After interviewing a student recently, he really responded to me. It has greatly improved our relationship.

These are the commonly volunteered references to what happens when thought-provoking questions are asked in an open, accepting manner and attended to by a perceptive listener who has the desire to help. Relationships are built and the heaviness of the unknown lifts. People come to know each other better and learning is facilitated.

Evolution of the SRI Process of Listening

The idea of a structured, low-stress interview as a way of discovering the uniqueness of individual students has roots deep in research that has extended over a time span of more than 20 years.

RESEARCH BASE

Early in the 1950s, Donald O. Clifton, now the president of Selection Research, Inc. (SRI) of Lincoln, Nebraska, had the responsibility for a counseling program at the University of Nebraska. The positive focus of the program was to alert underclassmen to the opportunities for development of their own potential. To do this, a counselor was to spend some time with each freshman student every week. In these meetings, they were to consider the freshman's development in all realms: academic, social, leadership, and creative capacity. Since there were not enough professional counselors to do this job, seniors and graduate students were selected.

After selection, counselors were trained and the program was begun. As the semester progressed, while some counselees were heard to say, "This is a waste of time," other students were saying, "This is the best experience I'm having on campus." In trying to assist persons who exhibited negative attitudes, a discovery was made. If a freshman was found who said it was a "waste of time" and others said the same thing, they would likely be going to the same counselors. On the other hand, if a freshman thought the program was great, other students going to the same counselor were also likely to be positive.

Clifton's observation was that the counselor *as a person* was making the difference. All that could be done in training was being done. For some, it helped, but for others it did not. The question was: How could you discover the unique talents of a person prior to selection? How might counselors who could develop an activating type of relationship with the counselee be identified?

PATTERNS OF THOUGHT

Clifton was advised by Gardner Murphy, who is a past president of the American Psychological Association, that personal values were likely to be the distinguishing features that would discriminate between the counselors who were succeeding and those who were not. Paper and pencil tests were used to test out this theory. The results were statistically significant but not predictive.

The researchers finally hit on the idea of studying tape recorded interviews to identify the counselor's thought patterns because they realized in talking to the counselors informally that they "talked differently." For example, counselors who had positive responses from students talked spontaneously about individuals, while counselors drawing more negative responses tended to discuss procedures.

These recurring patterns of thought later become known as *life themes*. The word themes is used to indicate a conceptual organization point. It should not be confused with a mathematically derived factor.

This discovery of differences in counselors led to other areas of study and an accumulation of experience in talent identification and predictive selection. A structured, low-stress process of *interviewing* proved to be a valuable tool in predicting behavior. Application of the process has been made in many areas such as sales, management, law enforcement, and denistry; but much of the early and continuing research has been in the area of education.

VALIDITY AND RELIABILITY STUDIES

Early studies established that the interview process had significant concurrent validity in predicting the effectiveness of teaching as judged by a teacher's students (Bonneau, 1956). The correlations were high and supported the prediction of teacher effectiveness from the interview results. A scorer reliability study showed high agreement between trained analysts.

G.W. Dodge studied the reliability of thought patterns that were elicited by the interview technique over a four-year period. He found remarkable similarity from year to year in the essential content of interviews with students enrolled in the Teachers College at the University of Nebraska. He discovered that the analysis of thought patterns of prospective teachers as college freshmen was more predictive of the ratings they would receive from their pupils during student teaching than other frequently used measures, such as grades, standardized tests, or supervisor's ratings (Dodge, 1964).

SRI Student Perceiver Interview Process

These research discoveries helped to establish a base for the SRI Student Perceiver Interview process. The 80-question Student Perceiver Interview can be administered to most students in approximately 30 minutes (if you choose to complete the entire set of questions). It is designed not as a test with "correct" and "incorrect" answers, but as a systematic process to provide student growth facilitators (teachers, counselors, psychologists, administrators, etc.) with a technique that can be used with success in perceiving the uniqueness of individual students, from age eight through adulthood. (Written permission from parents or guardians is usually secured prior to using the interview with underage students.)

The interview in the hands of a person competent to administer and interpret the results provides valuable assistance in identifying and developing student talent. It offers comprehensive data to better identify what the talents of students are, to better inform teachers about them so that individualized programs can be provided, and to help students better understand themselves.

The interview follows a format that allows the student to respond spontaneously in an open, accepting atmosphere. The interviewer is free to listen and perceive the presence or absence of the various life themes or thought patterns as well as discover the unique qualities of the interviewee.

THEMES OF SRI STUDENT PERCEIVER INTERVIEW

There are three major divisions of 16 themes within the SRI Student Perceiver Interview. The first set is referred to as *interactive*. These themes have to do with understanding the motivation of a person as he interacts with his environment and within his time space. The following qualities are examples of the interactive theme:

SUCCESS—The success theme is indicated when a person has experienced a great deal of success and readily refers to successes as a basis for present activities and for expecting a successful future. It is knowing you have talent and knowing how to express that talent in a way that is recognized positively.

FUTURISTIC—The thought processes of the futuristic person are regularly and spontaneously conceptualizing the future. The thought content reveals futuristic forecasts, dreams, and projections.

ACCOMMODATION—Accommodation is the ability to adjust to a seemingly adverse situation rather than overreacting. Accommodation is also the ability to give up a mediocre procedure in favor of one that would be more effective. Accommodation is a person's willingness to change, the ability to be flexible when appropriate.

The second division of themes is called *intrapersonal* because they point more to the qualities within the person. Examples are:

TIME BINDER—Signifies the ability to defer present gratification to a future time when a more sophisticated gratification may be experienced. A student is willing to study and learn the initial skills of a performance knowing that only at some future time will he be able to practice the total performance.

FOCUS—Denotes the ability to take a direction and maintain it.

The person with focus has plans and goals and can look to other people as models to emulate.

GESTALT—The tendency to perceive in terms of configurations, to have a need for closure and completeness. The person with high gestalt feels uneasy until things are organized or finished.

Interpersonal themes, designating a student's relationships with elements outside of himself, make up the third division. Examples are listed below:

PEER RELATIONSHIPS—The ability to establish a positive and mutually beneficial relationship with students and other peers.

ADULT RELATIONSHIPS—The capacity to relate positively with adults, especially teachers and parents.

POSITIVITY—Indicates a generally optimistic, favorable attitude toward people with whom he works. The person with this quality selects out and responds to the positive features of his social or physical environment.

LEARNING STYLE QUESTIONS

Information regarding the learning style of a student can be revealed anywhere in the interview; however, there are specific questions designed to allow the interviewees to talk about the "best ways" for them to learn something, while other items ask for references to their energy, punctuality, dedication to a task, neatness, past educational successes, specific areas of interest, goals, plans for the future, and other characteristics which influence their unique approach to learning.

Interview questions which can be asked comfortably in an educator/student conversation take three forms. *Situational* questions ask the student to react to a particular situation. *Observational* questions give the interviewee an opportunity to reflect on the actions of a third party. *Direct* questions ask students to indicate their own personal beliefs, feelings, and ideas.

SYSTEMATIC PROCESS OF LISTENING

The SRI Student Perceiver Interview is a *structured* interview. The "structure" requires the interviewer to:

- *Ask the questions using an exact wording.* If the wording is paraphrased, there is less basis for comparing one student with another student or group or with previous results on the same interviewee.

- *Ask the questions in the proper order.* Questions are so arranged that the interviewee does not respond to all five questions of a single theme in sequence. The questions rotate one per theme through all 16 themes until five questions have been asked about each. This way the interviewer can discontinue the interview at any point should time become a factor and still have evidence of the presence or absence of all themes.

- *Be a responsive listener.* Accept what the interviewee says. So often we are tempted to define terms and in a sense tell the student what we want him to say. A part of the structure is to resist this temptation to tell, to opt for the more helpful act of listening by not interrupting or giving personal opinions. Terms are defined only when absolutely necessary, thus allowing students to tell what they mean.

- *Resist probing or cross-examination.* The structured questions will reveal the interviewee's thought patterns and feelings. If the interviewer thinks of additional questions, they can be asked at the end of the structured interview. This avoids unnecessary tangents and saves time. Usually the interviewee provides a sufficient amount of information in answering prescribed questions.

- *Record the interview.* A tape recording of the interview ensures that the content of the responses will not be lost should the mind of the interviewer wander. The recording furnishes an opportunity to restudy the session for a more indepth analysis and frees the interviewer from having to take potentially distracting notes. A recording can even be scripted if literal accuracy is required.

LOW-STRESS INTERVIEW PROCESS

The structured format is designed to enhance the low-stress quality of the interview session. A statement like the following is used to introduce the session:

The major purpose of this interview is to get to know you better. I will be using what you tell me as information to help me help you learn and develop your talents as a person. Therefore, it is important for you to be honest and open with me and yourself as you respond to the questions.

The interview has some interesting and straightforward questions that you should enjoy answering. There are no right or wrong answers, so just tell it like it is. Give me your own answer, not what you think someone else wants you to say.

I will read the questions to you and then I will be listening to your answer. I can repeat a question whenever you want me to. We have plenty of time, and you may go back to previous questions any time you want to.

I may be making some notes as we go along, but I will mostly be listening to you. I will record our interview so I can go back and study it again if I need to.

Unless you have any questions for me, I'll turn on the recorder and we will get started.

The novice interviewer is usually surprised how relaxed the interviewee is during the session and how much valuable information is revealed. An inexperienced interviewer tends to expect that the structured procedure and the use of a tape recorder will inhibit the student. This has not been the experience. Interviewers report even after their first time using the process a feeling of closeness and understanding gained through careful questioning and listening.

To further assure the student that the session has been conducted in his own best interest, a statement like the following is used in closing:

Thank you for talking with me. I feel I know you a lot better now, and I think I have learned some things I can use to help you here in school. (Interviewer may want to give a positive example of something learned at this point.) I appreciate how open you were and how you shared your ideas with me. I may want to tell other teachers here at the school some of your interests, goals, and other things I have learned that will be helpful to you, if this is okay with you. Is there anything you have told me that you would not want me to tell anyone else? (Agree to the conditions.) Thank you. I will be talking to you later after I have had an opportunity to study your interview further.

STUDENT FEEDBACK

The feedback process and application of interview results varies with the original purpose of the interview. Sometimes the results are directly discussed only with the student. At times, parents and/or teachers may be included in the feedback session.

The sessions are positive in nature, largely because the questions and the themes the interviewer listens for are positive. Each question has a specific "listen for," a point of reference to focus the interviewer's attention on the particular theme so that interpretation may be more consistent.

The feedback session generally follows this sequence:

1. Starts by pointing out one discovery or positive characteristic the interviewer feels the best about.

2. Discussion of what the student can do—potentialities, commendable behavior, abilities, achievements, outstanding accomplishments, etc.

3. Discussion of what the student wants to do—needs, values, beliefs, interests, aspirations, desires, satisfactions, etc.

4. Discussion of how this student behaves—style, patterns, typical behavior, major theme strengths, etc.

5. Finally, the interviewer helps the student look ahead to plan how he can use the unique talent potential discovered through the interview and feedback process. Emphasis is on planning successes which will result in a fuller realization of potentiality.

Often during the feedback session, information from sources other than the interview (parents, teachers, records, observations, etc.) is also discussed in an effort to get an even more complete picture. The interview is not designed to stand alone. It should be considered along with achievement, aptitude, observed behavior, and other appropriate surveys.

Application and Results

An early version of the SRI Student Perceiver was field-tested at the Youth Development Center in Kearney, Nebraska, a special secondary school for boys sentenced by courts. In a similar school for girls, the interview was found to be predictive of recidivism (Dredge, 1973). The interview is now used at the Youth Development Center as a basis for designing individualized programs for students who are significantly low in basic reading and/or math skills. As a result of participating in individually designed programs, 95 boys with reading difficulties who were enrolled in the project over a two-year period gained an average of one year and one month on the Wide Range Achievement Test, in approximately one month's time. A total of 79 boys who were enrolled because of difficulties in mathematics showed the same rate of growth. Gains in the SRI Self-Concept as a Learner and SRI Attitude Toward School scales showed an increase of 25 percentile points and

23 percentile points, respectively, in an average of one month's time.

The SRI Student Perceiver Interview has been utilized in a wide range of educational settings: the vocational guidance program at the Ashland-Greenwood Public Schools in Nebraska; the special learning disabilities program at District #66 in Omaha, Nebraska; a tool for student growth facilitators in Holdrege, Minden, Kearney as well as York, Nebraska; a private elementary school (St. Rita's) in Aurora, Illinois; public schools in Security, Colorado; Rantoul, Illinois; Worthington, Ohio; West Bend, Wisconsin; and Saratoga, Wyoming, where specialists in the use of the process have been trained. It is being used to support efforts in individualized instruction in Sioux Falls, South Dakota, and as a focal point for counselors who are trying to lower the suspension and expulsion rate in three school districts in Louisiana.

COMPETENCY-BASED CERTIFICATION

The SRI Student Perceiver Interview is also proving to be a helpful basis for educator inservice training. The interviewer seems to gain a great deal both in personal growth and professional insight as a result of participation in the SRI training experiences. To be certified as a SRI Student Perceiver Specialist, the interviewer (often a teacher, counselor, or psychologist, but also at times an administrator or even an upper division student) participates in a competency-based training sequence. Training begins during an introductory seminar conducted in or near the school and is followed by a combination of correspondence and seminar experiences until proficiency is established in conducting, coding, and interpreting the interview. Certified Student Perceiver Specialists who achieve certain preestablished levels of reliability in the process are then authorized to train others within the school.

THE POWER OF AWARENESS

The real "magic" of the process is summarized in the following: "There is a power in the awareness of another person and his awareness of your awareness." The potential for individual growth is enhanced within a relationship of awareness; the SRI Student Perceiver Interview provides a unique vehicle for initiating a growth facilitating relationship.

The Boys Town slogan and Will Roger's philosophy come to mind again. It is easier to like and to help those you understand. A person

who takes the time to listen will begin to understand; and once understood the weight of the unknown lifts and the possibility of being
helpful becomes more likely. The SRI Perceiver Process is a valuable
tool to identify and develop the talents of individuals.

Chapter 8

The Other Difference
Between Boys and Girls

Richard M. Restak

Boys think differently than girls. Recent research on brain behavior makes that conclusion inescapable. Indeed, social equality for
men and women really depends on recognizing these differences in
brain behavior.

At present, schooling and testing discriminate against both boys and
girls in different ways, ignoring differences that have been observed by
parents and educators for years. Boys suffer in elementary school
classrooms, which are ideally suited to the way girls think. Girls suffer
later on, in crucial ways, taking scholarship tests that are geared for
male performance.

Anyone who has spent time with children in a playground or school
setting is aware of differences in the way boys and girls respond to similar situations. Think of the last time you supervised a birthday party
attended by five-year-olds. It's not usually the girls who pull hair, throw
punches or smear each other with food.

Usually such differences are explained on a cultural basis. Boys are
expected to be more aggressive and play rough games, while girls are
presumably encouraged to be gentle, nonassertive and passive. After
several years of exposure to such expectations, the theory goes, men
and women wind up with widely varying behavioral and intellectual
repertoires. As a corollary to this, many people believe that if child-
rearing practices could be equalized and sexual stereotypes eliminated, most of these differences would eventually disappear. As often
happens, however, the true state of affairs is not that simple.

Undoubtedly, many of the differences traditionally believed to exist
between the sexes are based on stereotypes. But despite this, evidence
from recent brain research indicates that many behavioral differences
between men and women are based on differences in brain function-

ing that are biologically inherent and unlikely to be modified by cultural factors alone.

Differing Sensitivities

The first clue to brain differences between the sexes came from observations of male and female infants. From birth, female infants are more sensitive to sounds, particularly to their mother's voice. In a laboratory, if the sound of the mother's voice is displaced to another part of the room, female babies will react while male babies usually seem oblivious to the displacement. Female babies are also more easily startled by loud noises. In fact, their enhanced hearing performance persists throughout life, with females experiencing a fall-off in hearing much later than males.

Tests involving girls old enough to cooperate show increased skin sensitivity, particularly in the fingertips, which have a lower threshold for touch identification. Females are also more proficient at fine motor performance. Rapid tapping movements are carried out quickly and more efficiently by girls than by boys.

In addition, there are differences in what attracts a girl's attention. Generally, females are more attentive to social contexts—faces, speech patterns and subtle vocal cues. By four months of age, a female infant is socially aware enough to distinguish photographs of familiar people, a task rarely performed well by boys of that age. Also at four months, girls will babble to a mother's face, seemingly recognizing her as a person, while boys fail to distinguish between a face and a dangling toy, babbling equally to both.

Female infants also speak sooner, have larger vocabularies and rarely demonstrate speech defects. Stuttering, for instance, occurs almost exclusively among boys.

Girls can also sing in tune at an earlier age. In fact, if we think of the muscles of the throat as muscles of fine control—those in which girls excel—then it should come as no surprise that girls exceed boys in language abilities. This early linguistic bias often prevails throughout life. Girls read sooner, learn foreign languages more easily and, as a result, are more likely to enter occupations involving language mastery.

Boys, in contrast, show an early visual superiority. They are also clumsier, performing poorly at something like arranging a row of beads, but excel at other activities calling on total body coordination. Their attentional mechanisms are also different. A boy will react to an inanimate object as quickly as he will to a person. A male baby will often ignore the mother and babble to a blinking light, fixate on a geometric figure and, at a later point, manipulate it and attempt to take it apart.

A study of nursery preschool children carried out by psychologist Diane McGuinness of Stanford University found boys more curious, especially in regard to exploring their environment. McGuinness' studies also confirmed that males are better at manipulating three-dimensional space. When boys and girls are asked to mentally rotate or fold an object, boys overwhelmingly outperform girls. "I folded it in my mind" is a typical male response. Girls, when explaining how they perform the same task, are likely to produce elaborate verbal descriptions which, because they are less appropriate to the task, result in frequent errors.

In an attempt to understand the sex differences in spatial ability, electroencephalogram (EEG) measurements have recently been made of the accompanying electrical events going on within the brain. Ordinarily, the two brain hemispheres produce a similar electrical background that can be measured by an EEG. When a person is involved in a mental task—say, subtracting 73 from 102—the hemisphere that is activated will demonstrate a change in its electrical background. When boys are involved in tasks employing spatial concepts, such as figuring out mentally which of three folded shapes can be made from a flat, irregular piece of paper, the right hemisphere is activated consistently. Girls, in contrast, are more likely to activate both hemispheres, indicating that spatial ability is more widely dispersed in the female brain.

Sex Bias in Tests

When it comes to psychological measurements of brain functioning between the sexes, unmistakable differences emerge. In 11 subtests of the most widely used test of general intelligence, only two subtests reveal similar mean scores for males and females. These sex differences have been substantiated across cultures and are so consistent that the standard battery of this intelligence test now contains a masculinity-feminity index.

Further support for sex differences in brain functioning comes from experience with subtests that eventually had to be omitted from the original test battery. A cube-analysis test, for example, was excluded because, after testing thousands of subjects, a large sex bias appeared to favor males. In all, over 30 tests eventually had to be eliminated because they discriminated in favor of one or the other sex. One test, involving mentally working oneself through a maze, favored boys so overwhelmingly that, for a while, some psychologists speculated that girls were totally lacking in a "spatial factor."

Most thought-provoking of all is a series of findings by Eleanor Maccoby and Carol Nagly Jacklin of Stanford on personality traits and intellectual achievement. They found that girls whose intellectual achievement is greatest tend to be unusually active, independent, competitive and free of fear or anxiety, while intellectually outstanding boys are often timid, anxious, not overtly aggressive and less active.

In essence, Maccoby and Jacklin's findings suggest that intellectual performance is incompatible with our stereotype of femininity in girls or masculinity in boys.

Research evidence within the last six months indicates that many of these brain sex differences persist over a person's lifetime. In a study at the University Hospital in Ontario that compared verbal and spatial abilities of men and women after a stroke, the women did better than men in key categories tested. After the stroke, women tended to be less disabled and recovered more quickly.

Research at the National Institute of Mental Health is even uncovering biochemical differences in the brains of men and women. Women's brains, it seems, are more sensitive to experimentally administered lights and sounds. The investigator in charge of this research, Monte Buchsbaum, speculates that the enhanced response of the female brain depends on the effect of sex hormones on the formation of a key brain chemical. This increased sensibility to stimuli by the female brain may explain why women more often than men respond to loss and stress by developing depression.

It's important to remember that we're not talking about one sex being generally superior or inferior to another. Rather, psychobiological research is turning up important functional differences between male and female brains. The discoveries might possibly contribute to further resentments and divisions in our society. But must they?

Changing the Schools

It seems to me that we can make two responses to these findings on brain-sex differences. First, we can use them to help bring about true social equity. One way of doing this might be to change such practices as nationwide competitive examinations. If boys, for instance, truly do excel in right-hemisphere tasks, then tests such as the National Merit Scholarship Examination should be radically redesigned to assure that both sexes have an equal chance. As things now stand, the tests are heavily weighted with items that virtually guarantee superior male performance.

Attitude changes are also needed in our approach to "hyperactive" or "learning disabled" children. The evidence for sex differences here is staggering: More than 95 percent of hyperactives are males. And why should this be surprising in light of the sex differences in brain function that we've just discussed?

The male brain learns by manipulating its environment, yet the typical student is forced to sit still for long hours in the classroom. The male brain is primarily visual, while traditional classroom instruction demands attentive listening. Boys are clumsy in fine hand coordination, yet are forced at an early age to express themselves in writing. Finally, there is little opportunity in most schools, other than during recess, for gross motor movements or rapid muscular responses. In essence, the classrooms in most of our nation's primary grades are geared to skills that come naturally to girls but develop very slowly in boys. The results shouldn't be surprising: a "learning disabled" child who is also frequently "hyperactive."

"He can't sit still, can't write legibly, is always trying to take things apart, won't follow instructions, is loud, and, oh yes, terribly clumsy," is a typical teacher description of male hyperactivity. We now have the opportunity, based on emerging evidence of sex differences in brain functioning, to restructure elementary grades so that boys find their initial educational contacts less stressful.

At more advanced levels of instruction, efforts must be made to develop teaching methods that incorporate verbal and linguistic approaches to physics, engineering and architecture (to mention only three fields where women are conspicuously under-represented and, on competitive aptitude tests, score well below males).

The second alternative is, of course, to do nothing about brain differences and perhaps even deny them altogether. Certainly there is something to be said for this approach too. In the recent past, enhanced social benefit has usually resulted from stressing the similarities between people rather than their differences. We ignore brain-sex differences, however, at the risk of confusing biology with sociology, and wishful thinking with scientific facts.

The question is not, "Are there brain-sex differences?" but rather, "What is going to be our response to these differences?" Psychobiological research is slowly but surely inching toward scientific proof of a premise first articulated by the psychologist David Wechsler more than 20 years ago:

"The findings suggest that women seemingly call upon different resources or different degrees of like abilities in exercising whatever it is we call intelligence. For the moment, one need not be concerned as to which approach is better or 'superior.' But our findings do confirm what poets and novelists have often asserted, and the average layman long believed, namely, that men not only behave, but 'think' differently from women."

This article is adapted from the author's book, The Brain: The Last Frontier, published by Doubleday.

Chapter 9

A Plan for Matching Learning and Teaching Styles

Wesley R. Anderson
S. William Bruce

The history of education is replete with movements that briefly influenced the course of the profession, and then passed on, leaving a legacy upon which researchers, philosophers and practitioners could build. As the literature on the subject of learning styles grows, it is becoming apparent that this is an idea that may join the select group of concepts that has had a major and lasting impact on education.

The idea of studying how humans learn is certainly not a new thing. What is new and refreshing is that the research on the information processing habits of learners has produced instrumentation that is useful in identifying specific learning styles. Identification of styles has led, in turn, to a new look at classroom activities in the light of students' learning characteristics.

The purpose of this chapter is to discuss the practical application of some of the work in learning styles. The authors acknowledge a debt to the NASSP Model Schools Project and to the Learning Environments Consortium for demonstrating that innovative programs can and should be implemented on a total basis rather than within a few rooms in a conventional school. It is this fact, so forcefully brought home by the Model Schools Project in particular, that now allows educators to work toward significant change without the fear of destroying a school's program and/or arousing the wrath of school patrons.

Description of the Project

Highland High School, Bakersfield, California, has had a measure of success in developing an individualized program of instruction but recently has found itself forced by financial considerations into a conventional, group-oriented curriculum. This change has caused problems in staff morale because the highly competent faculty could see several years of innovative work being discarded. It became necessary to search for ways to continue treating students as individuals while living within a drastically reduced budget. The literature on learning styles suggested the possibility of an approach that would support individualization of instruction for students who truly could profit from it along with other modes of instruction suggested by school, student, and teacher needs.

Principal's Role

The principal's role in the modern secondary school calls for educational leadership. The research establishes rather conclusively that curriculum change will be successful only if the principal takes an active leadership part in the program. At Highland, the principal undertook to achieve two primary instructional goals:

- To become as familiar as possible with the work done in the field of learning styles.
- To determine what staff development process would support a practical instructional program incorporating the learning styles concept.

After a review of the research and developing a skeleton outline of how the program should proceed, it became evident that this could not be a short-term project. It would obviously take a considerable amount of time to become familiar with the various alternatives advocated by different authors and to select an approach that would meet the problems of a comprehensive public high school. As a matter of fact, it was two years before the school was ready to set up a pilot program.

Selecting a group of staff members to work on the project was the first step. Asking for volunteers did not seem to be feasible. It was plain that the members of this group had to be people interested in and committed to applied research. The literature on learning styles is relatively complex and reading, discussing, and evaluating it requires both time and intellectual commitment. Consequently, specific staff members were approached and asked if they were interested in working on an implementation plan. Seven persons accepted the challenge and the Learning Styles Committee (LSC) was formed.

The LSC formulated an attack plan and requested two major logistical items: (1) a special budget and (2) the assurance that released time would be made available. The budget was intended for an ERIC search and the purchase of testing instruments. Released time was programmed into teachers' schedules so that the group could meet for discussion and planning.

The committee's plan included the following steps:

1. The acquisition of reading materials on learning style—a small, rather select professional library.

2. Discussion of the concepts and the development of a tentative plan of implementation.

3. The examination and piloting of testing instruments.

4. The identification of a student population to be included in the program, including the advisability of a pilot program and perhaps a "schools-within-a-school" structure.

5. Developing a process to keep the faculty informed of the committee's progress.

Structure and Definitions

Our initial plan incorporated a decision to structure the program as three schools within a school. The identification of student learning styles does not produce clear-cut categories but places subjects along a continuum (Witkin et al., 1971; Rotter, 1966). This argues for general grouping with a certain amount of variation within groups. It demands judgmental decisions of program administrators. Gradually the LSC became convinced that the "learning style" it was looking for was really a "learning profile" that encompassed many variables in the learning process. The committee accordingly began to conceptualize an individual's learning style as a profile of various psychological, intellectual, and personality variables.

Two main concepts were chosen as focal elements of the profile. The first was field dependence/field independence; the second, locus of control (internality/externality). There was also recognition that the LSC might be taking an overly simplistic approach to a complicated process, but it was necessary to keep in mind what was practical for a comprehensive public school.

A number of approaches were examined and particular attention, among others, was given to the instruments and procedures of Rita and Kenneth Dunn and Joseph Hill. The LSC carefully reviewed the somewhat lengthy Dunn instrument (Learning Style Inventory) and considered shorter versions as alternatives. Eventually the committee concluded that while these techniques may do a good job of identifying students' learning styles, the instrumentation involved was too demanding and expensive for a project such as this.

The term "learning styles" has come to include many variables in the learning process. Perhaps the most commonly accepted dimension is "cognitive style" defined as "information processing habits. . . . They are characteristic modes of operation which, although not necessarily completely independent of content, tend to function across a variety of content areas" (Messick, 1972, p. 67). "An individual's cognitive style is a basic intellectual determinant in his/her level of achievement or success in educational environments" (Letteri, 1976, p. 65). Of the major investigations of cognitive styles, Witkin's dimension of field dependence/independence has received the most attention from researchers over the last decade.

It is important to define precisely what we mean by the terms "field dependence/independence" and "locus of control." We accepted these definitions:

Field Dependence. A dimension of cognitive style that is characteristic of an individual who: tends to have difficulty separating field from ground; is inclined to respond to a stimulus as a whole; tends to be dependent on others; is socially oriented. The term is used interchangeably with the term global style. (Witkin, 1974)

Field Independence. A dimension of cognitive style that is characteristic of an individual who: can perceive items as discrete from their background; can reorganize an already organized field; can provide structure to unstructured material; tends to be articulate when describing himself and his experiences; and tends to be independent. The term is used interchangeably with the term analytic style. (Witkin, 1974)

Locus of control explains "a person's perception of his control in a situation and his beliefs regarding whether his behavior, skills, and/or internal dispositions determine the reinforcement he perceives in a situation" (Niederwerfer, 1975).

External Locus of Control. According to Rotter (1966), "When a reinforcement is perceived by the student as following some action of his own but (is) *not*. . . entirely contingent upon his action, then in our culture it is typically perceived as the result of luck, change, fate, or as under the control of powerful others. . . . We have labeled this as a belief in external control."

Internal Locus of Control. "If the person perceives that the event is contingent upon his own behavior or his relatively permanent characteristics," Rotter (1966) termed this as a belief in internal control.

Instrumentation

As the LSC screened available instruments for assessing learning styles, certain desirable parameters began to emerge. The committee decided that it wanted an instrument that would be both valid and practical for use in a large comprehensive high school. It must (1) have a firm research basis, (2) be relatively inexpensive, (3) be usable for group administration, (4) have appropriate reliability/validity co-efficients, (5) be relatively simple and quick to administer and score, and (6) provide stylistic differentiation along a continuum. Herman Witkin's *Group Embedded Figures Test* and Julian Rotter's *People In Society Scale* were judged to be most representative of these criteria.

GROUP EMBEDDED FIGURES TEST (GEFT)

The GEFT (Witkin, Oltman, Raskin, and Karp, 1971) is a paper-and-pencil test administered to determine a student's cognitive style, that is, how the student perceives and processes information. This test requires students to find eight simple geometric forms hidden within 25 progressively more complex figures and then to trace the outlines of the forms. Students are identified as field dependent or field independent on an 18-point continuum reflecting their degree of recognition of the embedded figures in the test. The GEFT is hand scored. A high score suggests an interpretation of field independence. The test identifies individuals along a continuum ranging from analytic on one end (high score) to global or nonanalytic (low score) on the other. Researchers have obtained consistently high validity and reliability scores on the GEFT. (Witkin et al., 1971).

PEOPLE IN SOCIETY SCALE (PSC)

Rotter's *People in Society Scale* was constructed to determine whether or not a person believed that rewards were contingent upon his own behavior (Rotter, 1971). The PSC, frequently referred to as Rotter's *Locus of Control Test,* is a paper-and-pencil test administered individually or in group sessions to determine the extent of a student's "internality or externality," that is, his perception either of being in control of his environment (and thus his life) or being controlled by it.

The PSC contains 29 items in a forced-choice format. The items represent an attempt to sample I/E beliefs across a range of conditions such as interpersonal situations, school, government, work, and politics. Low scores demonstrate feelings of internal control while higher scores are signs of external control (along a 23-point continuum). The PSC may be hand or machine scored. The reliability and validity is substantiated by abundant research. (Richards, 1978; Rotter, 1966)

LEARNING ENVIRONMENT SURVEY (LES)

We developed a local survey instrument to determine student preferences for selected learning environments. The questionnaire consisted of three possible learning environments or schools within a school represented by a list of 10 essential components reflecting open, modified (hybrid), or traditional settings. The students were instructed to read the descriptions of each type of learning environment carefully, to rank the three "schools," and to circle three components beneath the "school" of their first choice—the one that most appealed to them. The questionnaires were hand scored and frequencies tallied by computerized data processing.

Validation Study

As a direct result of its efforts, the LSC became aware that despite the persistent interest in individualization of instruction and personalized learning, there have been few systematic attempts to adopt methods of instruction for particular learning characteristics. A potentially valuable direction would be to establish the relationship between learning styles and teaching styles/modes of instruction. At the very least, one practical use of knowledge about the effects of teachers' and students' cognitive styles, studied in interaction, would be to provide teachers with information on how to match their teaching strategies with the learning needs of dissimilar students.

The LSC implemented a learning placement program (called the OHT) for the open, hybrid, and traditional learning environments envisioned in the program. The OHT was predicated on the belief that student placement in an instructional program should be based on the way individuals learn, and not on the supposed value of a given program or mode on instruction. A study was undertaken to validate the proposed placement program while, at the same time, determining the efficacy of locus of control and/or field dependence/independence as predictors of student achievement.

The learning style placement program (OHT) was piloted in the tenth grade class. Although the LSC originally intended to completely match the sophomore class with "appropriately determined" modes of instruction, the severe financial and political constraints imposed by the passage of Proposition 13 in California precluded such a thorough program. Instead, students were heterogeneously mixed in every classroom environment in order to evaluate definite match/mismatch situations.

The GEFT and the PSC had been administered to the entire group at the conclusion of their freshman year to profile learning style propensities. Students were then *randomly* assigned to one of the three distinct learning environments (open, hybrid, and traditional).

Finally, the LES was administered to each student to determine personal preference for the proposed learning environments.

THE LEARNING ENVIRONMENTS

Open—A classroom organization based on continuous progress within which learning is not measured by time but rather in terms of a series of mutually developed performance objectives toward which a student works. It recognizes the basic differences in student rates of learning by providing a wide variety of pace and content options. The schedule of the open environment is designed to give teachers and students as much freedom as is reasonable in the use of time, space, number of persons, and individual content.

Hybrid—A classroom organization which calls for classes of varying size, flexibility in instructional grouping and frequency of class meetings, and allows for team teaching. Decisions about the organization of instruction as well as other professional judgments are made by teachers.

Traditional—A classroom organization defined by its acceptance of essentially teacher-centered approaches to instruction, limited curriculum, and conventional approaches to student scheduling, classroom organization, and staff utilization. A conventional classroom organization is one in which a single teacher meets daily for one instructional period with the same group of students for the duration of the course. No flexibility of meeting time or size of group is permitted by the teacher.

Eight tenth grade English teachers were selected to operationalize the three environments. A minimum of nine periodic assessments were conducted by the Learning Styles Committee to ensure that the correct modes of instruction were being employed. At the conclusion of the semester, the English grade for each subject was added to the individual's profile sheet.

THE RESULTS

Program data were analyzed by computer with the following results:

1. Cognitive styles (field dependence/independence), locus of control, and the interaction of these two variables are appropriate determiners of a student's learning style. Students with an internal locus of control and students identified as field independent received higher English grades than their counterparts.

2. Matching students with selected learning environments is an efficacious means of increasing student achievement, particularly when the matching is conducted on the basis of a student's learning style.

3. When given the opportunity to select learning environments for study, students tend to choose more open environments than what is empirically indicated. Student preference for a program or environment is *unrelated* to achievement either individually or in interaction with any other variable tested.

4. It is important for teachers to develop more open learning environments and those activities and strategies that will help students to move toward a more internal locus of control.

Some Implications

The program and results reported here as part of a strategy for matching teaching/learning styles may well cause some skeptical readers to ask "so what?" Yet the authors feel that the results of this admittedly limited step in styles matching may have significant and far-reaching implications. Improvement in education results as educators consciously examine the needs of students and determine appropriate instructional treatments with specific objectives. Many types of alternative instructional procedures can be utilized. Learners can be subdivided according to different curricula, or the same curriculum along different instructional lines, or with different learning modalities, and so on. Careful attention to cognitive style and locus of control differences under more or less structured conditions, and detailed analysis of the problem-solving skills and strategies assumed for different learning tasks can facilitate better instructional procedures for each kind of student. Unless educators appreciate how powerful a psychological tool the matching of learning with teaching styles can be in motivating —or demotivating—the learner, they will not effectively overhaul our schools no matter what innovations are introduced.

If administrators and teachers are to do more than pay lip service to the concept of individualized instruction, they must begin to utilize the concepts of student learning style and teacher instructional style in educational program planning.

Chapter 10

Cognitive Mapping and Prescriptive Education

Gerald E. Kusler

You know, I've been trying to individualize in my Non-Western Culture class. I'm sure not excited about what's happening."

"Why?"

"Oh, a few of the kids grabbed a topic and settled right in and they're clearly learning more than I could give them. But the rest! Forget it! Some are still dinking around trying to find something to get into. A few are all over me like a fog wanting to know what I want. Others spend the whole period gabbing with someone else. I'm try-ing—you know, guiding but letting them do their own thing—but next year I think I'll bag the individualizing."

"I wish I could help, but I don't know how."

That oversimplified, overgeneralized exchange sadly represents both teacher misunderstanding of "individualizing" and our impotence in helping. We have exhorted teachers to fit their instruction to the needs of individuals. We have bought "canned" instructional packets and spent thousands on teacher time for "homemade" packets. We have stockpiled programmed materials. We have bought or leased hardware ranging from cassette recorders to computers for use in CAI. We have inserviced teachers on all of the above—and contract learning, cross-aged tutoring, listening skills, inquiry method, Socratic questioning—and on and on. But something is missing. More often than not the new method, the new materials are brought to the classroom and applied wholesale. There's not much "individuali-zation," but there is some variety and that alone is probably worth the cost.

Some teachers, all too few in high schools, have really tried to make some judgments about youngsters, then to select materials and methods to fit. Teachers aren't by nature or training recalcitrant. They

don't want to treat kids as numbers, and in their normal human interactions, they don't. So what's the problem?

One part of the problem is that many of us don't look at kids diag-
nostically. Many teachers announce that they never look at a youngster's folder. "I don't want to brand him; he gets a fresh start with me."
The teacher who says that operates with a different image-production
maybe. He "takes the student where he is" and uses only the information he discovers. The notion of diagnosing and prescribing is dim;
individualizing tends to mean letting the student have a say in what
or how he learns. Diagnosis, what there is of it, usually consists of naming what the youngster should have learned and has not.

A second and more important part of the problem is that, though
we have urged teachers to individualize, we have given them very
little to help them know the student *as a learner*. We give them test
scores which describe his achievement or suggest his capacity. We
give them past grades. We give them sociological and family data.
But we don't do much about saying, "Here's how he thinks and responds as one of those 25 kids in your class." Consequently, Sally's
English teacher is more likely to know that Sally had a 430 on the
SAT verbal and that her dad's a drunk than he is to know that Sally's
most likely to learn working in a quiet spot with help from someone
her own age.

Cognitive Style Mapping

The answer, an answer—at least part of an answer—could lie in a
relatively new activity called "cognitive style mapping." Now, don't
turn off! It's really not a mystery, it's pretty easy to do, and it does help
you to know a number of things about a student and how he learns.
Joseph Hill, former president of Oakland Community College, developed cognitive mapping as a diagnostic tool. It's been used heavily
at Oakland, less extensively in some other junior colleges, and experimentally in some elementary schools. We are in our fourth year with
it at East Lansing High School.

We use a relatively simple profile form that asks the student to respond to 224 descriptive statements (see Figure 1). The student indicates whether the statement is true for him most of the time, sometimes, or rarely. His responses are weighted and combined to yield
a profile of the student as a thinker, learner, and performer in school.
(A disclaimer is important: this is not a psychological test; it is a formal-
ized set of self-descriptive statements. It is more akin to the gathering
of statements and answers by a physician reaching toward a diagnosis
than to a normal school test.)

Cognitive Mapping

- If I hear the daily news on the radio, I understand it better than if I read it in the newspaper.
- I find it comfortable to add spoken or dictated numbers mentally.
- I prefer maps to verbal directions when I am going to a strange place.
- When I go shopping, I read the price of each item and keep a running total in my head.
- Random sounds interfere with my ability to concentrate.
- A story is easier to understand in a movie than in a book.
- When someone is frightened, I can be patient and calm rather than reply in anger.
- I would stop for a "STOP" sign any time even if there were no other person in sight.
- In group discussions, I assume the leadership to persuade the group to reach a decision.
- When shopping for clothes, I prefer having a friend along to help me make choices.
- I consult with my immediate family before making decisions.
- When given a job to do, I prefer to do it myself.
- I "play the devil's advocate" with people to force them to look at another point of view.
- I work best in an organized or structured situation.
- I like to figure out the way the parts of a whole fit together.

Figure 1. *Sample items from the Cognitive Style Inventory (Hill, 1972)*

When the student's responses have been weighted and arranged, they provide what we call a "map." (Actually, that's not the origin of the term "cognitive mapping": Hill explained that "mapping" is mathematician's language naming a function to do with sorting binary numbers.) Our map gives us a relatively quick, graphic view of a student's learning terrain.

For each of 28 learner characteristics, our profile indicates to what degree this component seems to be significant in the student's "cognitive style." There are actually 17 gradations of "importance," but we simplify it all into three levels: we say that a component is a "major" (true more than half the time), a "minor" (true less than half the time), or a "negligible" (rarely ever true). By portraying each component as a bar on a graph, we have an easy-to-read, visual display of the student's cognitive map. (See Figure 2.)

The components we consider fall into three major groups: how the student takes in and processes stimuli and information, how the student's learning is affected by others, and how the student reasons to conclusions. In the first are factors like the impact of spoken and written words and numbers, the response to sensory stimuli, the impact of setting, etc. In the second we learn to what degree the student is influenced by peers and by authority. And, in the last we get clues as to the student's modes of inference: does he most often reason through use of rules, through logical proofs, by comparing, etc.?

What we learn is often incredibly simple. A student is miserable in a class in which he is being required to find an area of interest, draw up a contract, and set and meet a time schedule. The teacher is proudly "individualizing" but becoming increasingly peevish toward this ungrateful youngster who won't dig in and do it right. The student can't identify the source of his anxiety and tends to blame the teacher. If the teacher had a cognitive style map for the student, he might have learned that the student shows extremely low on individuality and very high on the role of authority, that he is negligible in the area of making and keeping commitments, that he responds much more to spoken than to written words, that he is a low minor on meeting time expectations, and that he reasons most often by the application of rules.

A teacher knowing those facts about a student would surely do things differently. Most important, probably, he would understand the learner's frustration and be able to help him with it. In planning the assignment, the teacher would know that this youngster will have trouble, will need almost daily checking and goal setting, and will need encouragement. The student having reviewed his "map" with the teacher will understand the sources of his anxiety, will know that the assignment gives him a chance to strengthen some of his weaker learning components, and can be open about seeking help from his teacher.

Prescriptive Education

You'll notice that the "prescription" for the above youngster is not necessarily a change in assignment or the incorporation of different methods or materials. It could be. If the major target is that the student fully understand rules and concepts from a chapter in a driver's educa-

COGNITIVE LEARNING STYLE PROFILE

® 1975 East Lansing High School
East Lansing, Michigan 488_

STUDENT _____ COURSE _____ HR. _____ DATE_____

SCORE	ELEMENT	MEANING	NEGLIGIBLE		MINOR		MAJOR				
THEORETICAL			1	2	3	4	5	6	7	8	9
_____	T(AL)	SPOKEN WORDS	8-10	12-14	16-18-20	22-24-26	28	30-32	34	36	38-40
_____	T(AQ)	SPOKEN NUMBERS	8-10	12-14	16-18-20	22-24-26	28	30-32	34	36	38-40
_____	T(VL)	WRITTEN WORDS	8-10	12-14	16-18-20	22-24-26	28	30-32	34	36	38-40
_____	T(VQ)	WRITTEN NUMBERS	8-10	12-14	16-18-20	22-24-26	28	30-32	34	36	38-40
SENSORY			1	2	3	4	5	6	7	8	9
_____	Q(A)	SOUND OTHER THAN WORDS & NUMBERS	8-10	12-14	16-18-20	22-24-26	28	30-32	34	36	38-40
_____	Q(O)	SMELL	8-10	12-14	16-18-20	22-24-26	28	30-32	34	36	38-40
_____	Q(S)	TASTE	8-10	12-14	16-18-20	22-24-26	28	30-32	34	36	38-40
_____	Q(T)	TOUCH	8-10	12-14	16-18-20	22-24-26	28	30-32	34	36	38-40
_____	Q(V)	VISION (OTHER THAN WORDS & NUMBERS)	8-10	12-14	16-18-20	22-24-26	28	30-32	34	36	38-40
PROGRAMMATIC			1	2	3	4	5	6	7	8	9
_____	Q(P)	AUTOMATIC MOTOR RESPONSE	8-10	12-14	16-18-20	22-24-26	28	30-32	34	36	38-40
CULTURAL CODES			1	2	3	4	5	6	7	8	9
_____	Q(CEM)	EMPATHY	8-10	12-14	16-18-20	22-24-26	28	30-32	34	36	38-40
_____	Q(CES)	ESTHETICS	8-10	12-14	16-18-20	22-24-26	28	30-32	34	36	38-40
_____	Q(CET)	ETHICS	8-10	12-14	16-18-20	22-24-26	28	30-32	34	36	38-40
_____	Q(CH)	STAGED BEHAVIOR	8-10	12-14	16-18-20	22-24-26	28	30-32	34	36	38-40
_____	Q(CK)	BODY LANGUAGE	8-10	12-14	16-18-20	22-24-26	28	30-32	34	36	38-40
_____	Q(CKH)	PRACTICES MOTOR SKILLS	8-10	12-14	16-18-20	22-24-26	28	30-32	34	36	38-40
_____	Q(CP)	JUDGMENT OF PHYSICAL & SOCIAL DISTANCE	8-10	12-14	16-18-20	22-24-26	28	30-32	34	36	38-40
_____	Q(CS)	SELF UNDERSTANDING	8-10	12-14	16-18-20	22-24-26	28	30-32	34	36	38-40
_____	Q(CT)	MAINTAINS POSITIVE INTERACTIONS	8-10	12-14	16-18-20	22-24-26	28	30-32	34	36	38-40
_____	Q(CTM)	MEETS TIME EXPECTATIONS	8-10	12-14	16-18-20	22-24-26	28	30-32	34	36	38-40
CULTURAL DETERMINANTS			1	2	3	4	5	6	7	8	9
_____	A	ASSOCIATES	8-10	12-14	16-18-20	22-24-26	28	30-32	34	36	38-40
_____	F	FAMILY	8-10	12-14	16-18-20	22-24-26	28	30-32	34	36	38-40
_____	I	INDIVIDUALITY	8-10	12-14	16-18-20	22-24-26	28	30-32	34	36	38-40
MODALITIES OF INFERENCE			1	2	3	4	5	6	7	8	9
_____	D	DIFFERENCES	8-10	12-14	16-18-20	22-24-26	28	30-32	34	36	38-40
_____	L	APPRAISAL (USING M, D, & R TOGETHER)	8-10	12-14	16-18-20	22-24-26	28	30-32	34	36	38-40
_____	M	MAGNITUDE (CATEGORICAL REASONING)	8-10	12-14	16-18-20	22-24-26	28	30-32	34	36	38-40
_____	R	RELATIONSHIPS (OR SIMILARITIES)	8-10	12-14	16-18-20	22-24-26	28	30-32	34	36	38-40
_____	K	DEDUCTIVE REASONING PROCESS	8-10	12-14	16-18-20	22-24-26	28	30-32	34	36	38-40

Figure 2. East Lansing High School Cognitive Learning Style Profile

tion book, there's no reason not to get it to him in whatever form will work—and his map will help the teacher to find that form. Some are going to "get it" best if they can read it and talk to other kids about it. Some need to be left alone with the book. Some will do best listening to an audio tape while they follow along in the book. Some need to see a film or videotape illustrating the situations described in the book. Cognitive maps will help a teacher fit methods and materials to the student—a very important element in prescription. Cognitive maps will help youngsters to seek learning strategies best suited to their style—and there's nothing wrong with prescribing for oneself.

Some other examples: One cognitive map component has to do with what are called "automatic motor responses." Our driver education teachers have come to realize that a student scoring "negligible" in this area is the kind of person who has great difficulty listening to directions, steering the car, operating the accelerator, and looking ahead at the same time. Most often he has to look at his hands or feet as he performs newly learned operations. Now, teachers using cognitive maps help the student to understand what his difficulty is likely to be and they plan in advance more behind-the-wheel time, with much slower introduction of new operations. They used to discover the problem late, throw up their hands, and often fail the student.

Chemistry teachers were among the first in our school to use maps extensively. They started with a commitment to individualize standard Chem Study chemistry. They gave up more than a summer dividing the material into individual packets with objectives, activities, and sets of tests. They put material on audio tape, sound page units, and film loops. They were thorough and committed. Yet, within a few weeks of the opening of school the complaints started rolling in. "I can't learn that way." "Those teachers are paid to teach: make them do it."

What happened was that for some kids, the new approach was a turn on. For others, many of them good students, it was a major frustration. We struggled along, reminding ourselves that many people resist change and that it wasn't surprising that some kids didn't like being made more responsible for their own learning. Time passed, but the complaints didn't. Then, our teachers began learning about cognitive style. They began mapping chemistry students and developing prescriptions. They learned many things and they have changed.

Some kids who learn best by reading, even reading a standard text, were wasting their time and growing frustrated trying to learn from audiovisual machines. Some kids who really need to hear an organized explanation by the "expert" were being deprived. Mini-lectures were scheduled for those people. Some youngsters do learn most efficiently if they can work with peers, but they were sitting at "study tables" wasting their time. Grouping had to be done differently and high school students assigned as aides had to assume new roles. As kids began to know their own maps they sought the best environment and strategies for learning. One student would say, "We know I have to keep checking out what I'm doing with you, Mrs. McGrain, but I'm doing better. This is the first time this week." While another student, working with the teacher, would be brought to understand that it's not his style to check his progress with anybody. Because the result could be misdirection and waste of time, the two would make a simple contract: "At least once a week we'll look over your work together." Some kids could accept or develop goals covering many weeks and stay right on schedule. Others would find only confusion or anxiety in such extended planning. When forced to do long-range planning, they would come up with unrealistic schemes. They had to start with daily goals. A cognitive style map helps them and their teachers to understand that, to plan for it, and to avoid the agony and time-wasting of discovery.

One last anecdote about chemistry: In a recent graduating class, there was a young woman who was mapped as a junior in the chemistry class. Throughout her high school experience she was known to both students and adults as a person with no social skills, no concept of her impact on others, and no capacity for empathy. She had trouble learning and she blamed her teachers, the school, the system. Authority figures—teachers, principals, parents—were odious to her. Her map, in relatively non-judgmental ways, helped her to begin to see these things about herself. Patiently, slowly, always in the context of helping her to learn, the teachers, counselor, and materials specialist helped her to know her style, then helped her with plans to augment it. There was no miraculous change. She did all right in chemistry . She seemed a bit less noticeable in the halls. Then, her senior year, we began to see the change. I first noticed it when I saw her start to shout after someone in the hall. She stopped, then hurried down the corridor, caught up with the girl and walked along talking quietly. A few weeks later, for the first time in her years in high school, she smiled at me and said, "Hi!" Teachers began talking about the change. By spring, we all saw her as a new person. The hostility was gone. On commencement night, when she began her walk across stage, she stopped, walked over to her chemistry teacher and embraced her. The girl made the change—not the cognitive style map— but beyond doubt the map did start it all.

Some Important Strategies

This anecdote offers a reminder of some important aspects about mapping. First, *it's something we do with kids, not to them.* Before we begin interpreting a map and making prescriptions based on it, we validate that map with the student. Usually in pairs—an administrator and a teacher, a teacher and a counselor, two teachers—we go over each item with the learner. We suggest meanings, ask questions, give examples. The learner responds. Usually, he says things like, "Boy, is that ever true!" and goes on to give examples. Occasionally, he gives us information and interpretations which cause us to alter the original profile. In any case, it's the learner's map and he knows it.

Second, *there are no goods and bads, no rights and wrongs.* To be "negligible" on willingness to practice motor skills is not to be wrong or inadequate. Knowing that this is part of my style, I'll do some things differently. If I want to learn a new skill, I'll avoid some grand practicing scheme. I'll stick to short practice sessions and I'll try to set it up so that I get some sense of growth or positive reenforcement each time. And, I'll tell someone who matters to me what I'm committing myself to because another part of my style is that commitments are of major importance to me. We try during the whole validation process and thereafter to stress the fact that majors aren't good things and negligibles bad ones. The map is a map, not a measurement. I suspect that one reason mapping seems to work with many youngsters is that so much of school is grading and measurement that anything which doesn't grade has an instant appeal.

Third, *a cognitive style map portrays the way it is now.* There's nothing inevitable about it; nothing saying, "This is the way you are and will always be.'" It does give the teacher and the learner some pretty clear indications about how the youngster is likely to learn best. Often, the wisest strategy will be to build learning activities on the strengths, the majors. But simply to say, "That's where he is, so we'll forget the rest" is absurd. Perhaps the student is a major in getting information through the spoken word and a low minor in intake from the written word. Surely, we'll not recommend that he quit reading! In fact, we give a lot of our attention to what we call "augmenting the map." The majors a student has, the more learning strategies are available to him. Therefore, the immediate strategy might call for learning the immediate subject by working with the major, but long-range plans would include activities to build some selected minors.

We have much yet to do. In our case, we have to reassure many teachers that they do not need to learn a whole, new, technical vocabulary and that they're not alone and don't have to be. We have to learn how to build effective prescriptions and to monitor them. We have to look for alternative ways to develop the profile and to show augmentation. We have to build a learning assistance center full of materials so that if one way to learn doesn't work we have alternatives ready.

Having been in education for many years, I've learned how addicted we are to fads. I want to believe that this is not another fad, that developing skills diagnosing learning styles and prescribing programs will really make a difference—for teachers, for kids, for schools. The signs are good.

Chapter 11

Meeting the Needs of Individuals Through Their Learning Styles

David P. Cavanaugh

Worthington High School in Worthington, Ohio, has developed two important overall goals for its educational program. They are:

- To provide throughout the school a wholesome, stimulating, productive, and satisfying learning environment conducive to the academic achievement and personal growth of individual students and staff members.

- To provide that all students and staff members, everyday, learn and grow and feel like human beings.

These goals were established several years ago as the result of two extensive inservice projects completed in the high school. The Indicators of Quality Project provided a measurement of interpersonal relationships between students and students, students and staff, and staff and staff. A subsequent School Climate (Humane) Improvement Project dealt with an assessment and analysis of the school's climate as well as the improvement of those factors that determine the quality of the climate.

While these projects dealt extensively with the affective domain, the cognitive domain was emphasized in the development and/or revision of curriculum, graded courses of study, and criterion-referenced testing.

The commitment to achieving productivity along with a sense of satisfaction in both students and staff led to a continuing search for a process which would enhance student learning. Some basic questions began to emerge with a high degree of frequency. How do students learn? What affects a student's ability to learn? What can the staff do to help students learn?

Staff members reviewed the literature and attended workshops that dealt with learning. The research and articles by Rita and Kenneth Dunn on learning styles and the work of the late Joseph Hill, *et al,* on cognitive mapping appeared to complement our objectives. Their work dealt directly with our questions on student learning. The Learning Style Inventory approach is essentially an instructional tool which can be employed by a classroom teacher who is attempting to individualize. Cognitive Style Mapping appeared to be a technique that could be better utilized by members of our guidance department in their attempts to help students and staff.

We administered the CSM inventory to all students in the fall of 1978 to provide information for guidance counselors to use in their work with students. At the same time, we agreed that participation in the LSI process would be strictly voluntary. Faculty members wishing to administer the LSI to their classes would be granted permission but participation in the process would carry with it certain obligations. Those teachers using the LSI would meet as a group once a month to share successes, strategies, and setbacks in an attempt to tie instructional strategy and environment to students' learning styles.

Forty-two faculty members (out of a staff of 145) volunteered to work with the learning style process. They agreed not only to meet monthly with the principal, but also on their own time with no extra pay or released time, to participate in inservice on learning styles prior to administering the inventory to their students. During the inservice program, we provided staff members with feedback on their own learning styles. In learning about themselves, the WHS staff members developed an awareness which was later to be helpful in learning about their pupils.

A Two-Pronged Approach

Some challenging problems arise in attempting a two-pronged approach to learning styles diagnosis (CSM and LSI). The first involves training the staff in the use and interpretation of existing instruments.

If the guidance counselors were to use cognitive mapping in their department, they would need help in developing awareness and skills in the use of this tool. The writing of Joseph Hill and others at Oakland Community College provided us with much information and direction. Gerald Kusler, principal of East Lansing High School in Michigan, conducted a one-day workshop for our guidance staff. This sharing provided a foundation for our own inservice dealing with terminology, interpretation, validation, and negotiation of prescriptions. The problem of implementing the CSM component, then, was met by researching the literature, by inservice and sharing with friends at East Lansing

High School, and by many long sessions with counselors in our own school.

The problems encountered in implementing the other prong of our approach—the Learning Style Inventory—were mostly of an educational nature. The staff had to be thoroughly educated in the LSI philosophy. An awareness was needed to allow each involved staff member to move from a global (undefined) acknowledgment that all students are different, to a specific, focused understanding of those differences in each student. Each staff member was given pertinent literature, opportunities for discussion and inservice, and exposure to a learning styles conference outside the school.

Staff Development

Staff members who volunteered for the program received strong support and encouragement from the principal. The principal also modeled the process in the classroom and led a monthly inservice program.

The agenda included these activities:

1. Sharing of successes
2. Diagnostic exercises
   a. Staff rotates in simulation of role
   b. Critique from group
3. Teaching of a method by staff volunteer
   a. Small groups—team learning;
      Circle of knowledge; brainstorming;
      case study
   b. Contract activity packages
   c. Programmed learning
   d. Instructional packages
      (1) Tactile materials
      (2) Kinesthetic materials
4. Questions to consider

The ability of the staff to develop an awareness of individual differences and to particularize those differences was our expectation for the first year. We accomplished that and more. The staff development program centered around the concept of student differences. There were a number of inservice objectives:

- To understand differences
- To develop strategies to diagnose differences

- To develop ability to prescribe for differences
- To develop skills to write programs which will be complementary to individual differences.

Except for attendance at learning style workshops conducted by the Dunns, all of the above was accomplished in-house. The monthly inservice meeting was the key to the whole process. Through these sessions the staff not only developed an awareness and the skills needed to individualize, but a sense of teaming and commitment grew day by day.

Current Developments

In working with the LSI this past school year (1978-79), we had several interesting experiences encourage us in our work with individual learning styles.

The administration of the LSI has evoked some curious student reactions. Teachers when giving the LSI had been asked to provide each student with a copy of the inventory questions. Teachers read the questions aloud to their classes, pausing after each question to provide time for the students to answer. We repeatedly found that three things happened:

- Some students listened to the teacher, ignored their own question sheets and then answered the question;
- Some students listened to the teacher while reading their question sheets before answering;
- Some students ignored the teacher entirely, read their question sheets, marked their answer sheet, and generally finished early.

This experience indicates to us that students, when given the opportunity, will use their most compatible learning styles. We will continue to observe this process as we administer the LSI next year.

We developed a Methods-Factor Coordination Sheet, which we are using to match learning styles to instructional methods (see Figure 1). Each staff member uses this guide to determine which program best fits his students. The factors are listed in an order of priority as they relate to differing methods. Recently we upgraded this technique by using the school computer to sort the matrix of methods and factors (see Figure 2). This allows us to print out, by computer, not only the learning style factors but also a suggested prescription by subject for each student (see Figure 3 for a sample printout). Note the relationship between "Susie Jones'" printout and the methods suggested on the Methods-Factor Coordination Sheet in Figure 2. More work is needed to refine this approach, but there is no question that it adds great flexibility to the processes of diagnosis and prescription. To enhance this flexibility, Worthington High School has scored the Learning Style Inventories on its own computer and provided each teacher with:

- The learning style factors for each student,
- A subscale showing the percentage of students relating to each factor,
- A list of all students indicating which factors are important to each.

By way of summary, we believe we are engaged in an exciting endeavor. The goals of Worthington High School commit us to provide an environment in which all students can learn and grow toward their greatest potential. We realize that this is a never-ending process. Therefore, it is our belief that developing a diagnostic/prescriptive approach to school learning which will provide for individual learning styles should be a minimum expectancy for all teachers and their students.

Figure 1. *Worthington High School methods factor coordination sheet*

Methods-Factor Coordination Sheet

Methods	*Compatible learning style factors (in priority order)*
Contract Activity Packages or Programmed Learning	1. Need for Structure 2. Visual/Tactual and Kinesthetic Appeals/Stimuli 3. Need to Work Alone
Instructional Packages	1. Tactual/Kinesthetic Appeals 2. Need for Structure Highly motivational resource, thus sociological stimuli may not matter 3. Need to Work Alone or Teacher-oriented
Task Cards and Learning Circles	1. Tactual and/or Kinesthetic Appeals 2. Visual Appeals
Lecture	1. Auditory Appeals 2. Teacher-motivation (adult) 3. Self-motivation 4. Need for Structure (tendency)

Figure 2. *Worthington High School Computerized M.F.C.S.*
Matrix

Methods-Factor Coordination Sheet

Methods	*Factors*
	Needs Structure or Not
	Auditory
	Visual
	Motivated or Not
	or
	Needs Structure or Not
Contract Activity Package	Auditory
Lecture (alternately)	
Limited Use of Task Cards	
and Tactual Materials	Self or Teacher-Motivated
Tapes; Audio Cassettes	
	Persistent
	Responsible
	or
	Needs Structure or Not
	Visual
	Self or Teacher-Motivated
	Persistent
	Responsible

Figure 2: *(continued)*

Methods	*Factors*
Programmed Learning *Task Cards and Other* *Tactile Materials* *Learning Circles* *Small Groups - if peer* *oriented*	Needs Structure Tactile-Kinesthetic Visual or Needs Structure Tactile or Kinesthetic Auditory
Instructional Packages *Task Cards and Other* *Tactile Materials* *Learning Circles* *Small Groups - if peer* *oriented*	Needs Structure Tactile or Kinesthetic Not Auditory Not Visual or Needs Structure Not Tactile or Kinesthetic Not Auditory Not Visual
Lecture *Tapes, Audio Cassettes*	Needs Structure Auditory Motivated Does *not* Need Mobility

Figure 3. *Worthington High School sample M.F.C.S. Printout*

Smith, John Dr.   Physics 2

Susie Jones   101178   Consistency Score 1.00
Id. No.   0   Gr. 12   W   F

Learning Style

Learning Style   LSI Reference Manual

3.	Requires bright light	Page 1
6.	Needs warm environment	Page 1
8.	Requires informal design	Page 1
10.	Adult-motivated	Page 1
11.	Teacher-motivated	Page 1
13.	Persistent	Page 2
15.	Responsible	Page 2
17.	Needs structure	Page 2
19.	Prefers learning alone	Page 3
25.	Has auditory preferences	Page 3
26.	Has visual preferences	Page 4
29.	Requires food intake	Page 4
31.	Functions best in morning	Page 4
36.	Does not need mobility	Page 4

Prescription:
Contract activity packages
    Lecture (alternately)
    Limited use of task cards and tactile materials
    Tapes; audio cassettes

Chapter 12

Using Learning Style Data to Develop Student Prescriptions

Rita Dunn
Kenneth Dunn

What kind of program is best for students?

- Structured or Open?
- Basic or Progressive?
- Traditional or Alternative?
- Subject-Oriented or Student-Oriented?

Falling into the educational label trap is at least as dangerous as it is misleading. The generalized "conservative" versus "liberal" tag is a handy yardstick misused by both critics and supporters of educational programs whether they are new or old.

As teachers and administrators we become the rather easy targets of self-proclaimed pied-pipers who would have us, in turn, follow a new math program here and retreat to basic computation skills there; embrace contextual linguistics then and rediscover phonics now. We are turned back and forth like heads at an exciting tennis match, waiting for the proponent or the critic to score a telling point and capture the bewildered majority watching the game.

The way for each youngster to win involves one attitude change and one action commitment.

Attitude: Draw a firm resolve to avoid the either-or, win-lose, your side-my side, correct-incorrect program controversy. The truth is that many of the current educational programs, if done well, will work if the student and program are properly matched. Most programs represent a basic philosophy which assumes that many youngsters learn in a pattern represented by that approach. Whether that philosophy and the teaching methods it advocates are good for individuals depends solely on the way(s) in which each youngster learns most easily. How a person learns is called his "learning style," and it is important to match correctly that style with the appropriate program for him.

How will you know if the fit is right? If your attitude has broadened beyond the stereotype that certain programs are either "good" or "bad," you can identify those that are very appropriate (perhaps ideal) and those that are just plain wrong for a given student and others who learn as he does.

Action: Read this chapter and its tables; become knowledgeable about the programs that have received the labels. Measure the underlying philosophy of each against your own. Observe classes within your own school (and others if possible) and use the descriptions and scales here as your first map of exploration. Gradually the terrain will become familiar and you will begin to recognize the teaching patterns and organizational landmarks of different schools.

Tables 1-4 outline the current in-vogue programs, their philosophies, and how students must behave to achieve academic success in each. Next to the "required-behaviors" column is a description of those behaviors translated into learning style traits. These explanations are not intended to promote one program over another. It is necessary to understand that each student learns in ways that are often extremely different from those of other persons, and that generally each program proves advantageous to one learning style. Of greater importance is the reality that no program can respond sensitively to every learning style. Should a youngster be placed in the wrong program for him, his ability to progress academically will be severely hampered (Dunn and Dunn, 1977).

Styles and Specific Strategies

It is important to remember that all four programs described in these tables are different from each other and provide generally discrete types of learning environments. They should not be confused with each other, although some teachers tend to use selected aspects of each, often inappropriately, because each represents a separate philosophy of how people learn. Since students learn in a variety of ways, each program serves strong needs of certain youngsters. No single program is appropriate for all (or even most) learners.

The placement of students should be based on the ways they learn, and not on the supposed value of a given program. For example, a high school student may be admitted to an alternative program because he volunteers (without having experienced it), cajoles or browbeats his parents into granting permission, or is not succeeding in the regular program. The alternative may be inappropriate for him if it requires skills and behaviors he cannot demonstrate like persistence ("follow-through") or alertness early in the morning. There are many considerations for admission into innovative programs, but self-selection and parental consent are only two of them. Of greater concern is the question, "Does this program make best use of the individual's learning style?"

Unfortunately, the reverse occurs too often. Students are required to adjust their learning styles to whatever teaching approaches are used. This may be damaging to their progress because it makes learning more difficult than it should be, causes frustration, and decreases a youngster's confidence in himself. Conversely, when a student learns in ways that are natural for him, the outcomes usually are increased academic achievement (Martin, 1977; Trautman, 1979), improved self-esteem (Hudes, Saladino, and Siegler, 1977), a liking for learning (Dunn and Price, in press), improved basic skills (Dunn and Dunn, 1978), stimulated creativity, and gradually increasing learner independence. Although it may be possible to teach students to become more effective learners through specific learning strategies (Weinstein, 1978), the outcomes are more likely to be positive if we teach them through their individual learning style characteristics.

During the years in which we worked to identify the scope of individual differences, we also experimented with a variety of resources to determine whether any relationship existed between specific learning style elements and materials through which students learn. Continuing study is necessary, but we have found that for the most part students with certain characteristics do tend to respond to selected resources. Table 5 enumerates some of the more popular methods and resources being used in schools and the learning style characteristics to which they (1) appear to respond, (2) apparently do not respond well, and (3) can be accommodated (Dunn and Dunn, 1978).

The information cited in Table 5 has been verified through extensive observation and study, but exceptions do occur where specific topics motivate students or when new resources cause a Hawthorne effect during the initial period of usage.

Learning About Students in Your School

Whatever the educational program—labeled or unlabeled—and the methods or resources, both administrators and teachers should be aware that students succeed best by utilizing their own most natural learning styles. If you want students to achieve, be certain that they are diagnosed accurately and prescribed for appropriately.

(cont. p. 122)

Table 1: Instructional Program: Traditional Classroom

Philosophy:

The teacher is responsible for helping students to achieve minimal grade-level standards. Students are expected to "pay attention," "try," "work," "take their work seriously," and "behave"—all of which presupposes that everyone is able to achieve through the method(s) selected by the teacher. Most of the instruction is through lecture and questioning, occasionally supplemented by media. Lesson plans are written by the teacher for the principal as indications of what the class will be taught. Grades are determined by the student's achievement on group tests. All students learn sequential blocks of subject matter at the same time. A few students are permitted some enrichment if it does not interfere with the curriculum to be covered. For all, self-selection of subject content and method of learning are rare.

Required Student Skills	*Learning Style Characteristics*	*Teaching Style Characteristics*
The student is required to:	The student should therefore:	The teacher:
1. pay attention for consecutive intervals of 20-50 minutes each.	be motivated.	is whole-class lesson oriented.
2. sit still for consecutive intervals of from one to three hours.	not require mobility.	essentially dominates the instruction or lesson.
3. refrain from needing a drink, a break, or using a lavatory except during specified times (recess, lunch, etc.).	not require intake, except at "correct" times.	is unaware of individual physical needs.
-or-	-or-	-or-
personally request permission to do any of the above during instructional time.	not be embarrassed because of being different from peers.	is structured and directive.
4. concentrate on studies for several hours during the school day and engage in homework after school.	be persistent.	is concerned with how much students learn.
5. retain information by listening.	be an auditory learner.	is lecture- and whole-class oriented.

Table 1 (continued)

Required Student Skills	Learning Style Characteristics	Teaching Style Characteristics
The student is required to:	The student should therefore:	The teacher:
6. learn at a table and chair or desk.	function easily in a structured environment.	employs rigid and traditional physical arrangements.
7. learn at his desk wherever it has been placed.	be unaffected by sound, light, and temperature.	assigns seats.
8. accept that what is taught is necessary, valuable, and interesting.	be authority-oriented.	is oriented to group and grade-level standards and content.
9. conform to externally established standards and rules.	be authority-oriented.	dominates instruction and behavior.
10. accept being marked on a competitive basis regardless of inherited ability or environmental background.	be authority-oriented.	employs group and grade-level standards.
11. learn whenever a subject is being taught.	be unaffected by time.	uses scheduled lesson plans.
12. keep working at an item until it is mastered.	be persistent.	focuses on sequenced material that must be covered.
13. maintain a positive self-image while following directions, maintaining self discipline, learning in a way that prohibits use of personal learning style, studying what may be irrelevant and uninteresting, and avoiding conflict.	be authority-oriented.	is authoritarian to reach class or grade-level objectives.

Table 2: Instructional Program: Individualized Classroom

Philosophy:

The teacher is responsible for diagnosing, prescribing for, and guiding each student through the learning process. Recognizing the different elements of learning style, the teacher permits students to work anywhere in the environment, in any sociological pattern that they choose. When a student evidences his ability to follow objectives that have been assigned to him, he is permitted to continue working as he prefers and is gradually permitted more and more options in objectives, resources, activities, and evaluation. When a student does not appear to be able to work independently, structure is added to his prescription so that he works to varying degrees under the direct supervision of the teacher. Multimedia, multisensory resources are available to students who may select from among them. Objectives are written on an individual basis and may be contributed to or developed by the student. When progress is not satisfactory, the teacher becomes increasingly directive. Grades are determined as a result of criterion-referenced testing related to each youngster's enumerated objectives.

Required Student Skills	Learning Style Characteristics	Teaching Style Characteristics
The student is required to:	The student should therefore:	The teacher:
1. identify those objectives, resources, activities, and assessment devices that need to be fulfilled. This will be done personally by students who can function independently and with the teacher by students who need guidance.	be permitted more options when he demonstrates responsible behavior and fewer options when he is unable to make choices that lead toward academic progress.	engages in diagnostic and prescriptive teaching.

Table 2 *(continued)*

Required Student Skills	Learning Style Characteristics	Teaching Style Characteristics
The student is required to:	The student should therefore:	The teacher:
2. identify the resources through which his objectives may be achieved. These will be itemized by the student. When student progress is not apparent or appropriate, resources will be prescribed by the teacher.	learn through resources that complement his perceptual strengths.	provides appropriate multisensory resources at various levels to facilitate the instructional planning.
3. complete individual prescriptions. When this is not done, the instruction will become formalized and more traditional. As the student evidences achievement, options in the mode of instruction will become available. As options increase achievement should continue to grow.	be given long-term prescriptions when he is motivated and/or persistent and short-term prescriptions when he does not follow through on prescriptions successfully.	is a manager of the teaching-learning process and is flexible and guiding with some students and directive and authoritarian with others.
4. self-assess his progress. Students who are able to evaluate their academic growth objectively are permitted to continue doing so. Students who are unable to do so are evaluated by the teacher frequently.	be assigned evaluation procedures that correspond to his ability to self-assess his growth.	uses different types of assessment devices with different types of students.

Table 3: Instructional Program: Open Classroom

Philosophy:

Students are permitted to determine their curriculum, resources, schedule, and pacing. They may remain with a topic as long as it interests them and may study alone, with a friend or two, or in a small group. Since students learn in very individual ways, the teacher is responsible for providing an environment rich in multimedia resources and encouraging student involvement with the materials. Objectives, if used, are determined by the learner and may vary from student to student and on a continuously changing basis. Grades are not given, but evaluations are made in terms of demonstrated growth. A positive and "happy" attitude is considered very important for student progress.

Required Student Skills	Learning Style Characteristics	Teaching Style Characteristics
The student is required to:	The student should therefore:	The teacher:
1. learn without continuous direction and supervision.	be motivated.	provides multiple resources.
2. avoid primarily social, rather than academic, experience.	be responsible.	permits wide options to students to learn and produce as they choose.
3. discipline himself to concentrate and to learn self-selected ideas, data, and values.	be motivated and responsible.	believes in students designing their own studies.
4. study in the midst of movement, discussion, and varied activities.	be unaffected by sound, structure, and the mobility of others.	believes in varied, continuing, interactive learning activities.
5. interact positively with others.	be peer-oriented.	provides varied options for working with one or more peers.
6. retain information without drill reinforcement.	have no need of imposed structure.	believes that students want to learn and will study as much as they are able.

Table 4: Instructional Program: Alternative Programs

Philosophy:

Students are given curriculum choices, decision-making responsibilities, and selected and optional objectives and are expected to gather and retain information independently. Students are usually permitted a voice in their program development. Since alternative programs differ widely, the degree to which options are provided in objectives, resources, activities, and evaluation is dependent on the individual program, not the student.

Required Student Skills	Learning Style Characteristics	Teaching Style Characteristics
The student is required to:	The student should therefore:	The teacher:
1. learn without continuous direction and supervision.	be motivated.	provides multiple materials and serves as a resource person or guide.
2. determine the scope, sequence, and depth of undertaken studies.	be responsible.	believes in student selection of objectives and procedures.
3. self-assess his progress and potential accurately.	be objective about self.	supervises self-evaluation by student.
4. discipline himself to study and achieve.	be motivated and responsible.	develops student self-reliance through consultation.
5. retain information without drill reinforcement.	have no need for imposed structure:	provides opportunities for independent study, individual or small-group assignments, other self-instructional materials and reinforcement procedures.

Table 5: Methodologies and Styles

Method or Resource	Brief Description	
1. Programmed Learning	*Linear Programming*	*Intrinsic Programming*
	This type of programming presents material in a highly structured sequence. Each part of the sequence is called a "frame," and each frame builds upon the one immediately preceding it. Each frame ends with an item that requires an answer—either in completion or multiple choice formats. Prior to the introduction of each subsequent frame, the answer to the previous frame is supplied. Program efficiency increases when the correct answer is accompanied by an explanation. Additional comprehension is developed when the incorrect answers also are accompanied by explanations.	Intrinsic programming also presents material in a highly structured sequence, but the major difference between linear and intrinsic types is that the intrinsic does not require each student to complete every frame. Intrinsic programming recognizes that some youngsters can move through learning experiences faster than others can, and it permits those who score correct answers to skip over some of the reinforcement frames. When students may bypass frames that teach the same aspect of a subject, the system is called "branching." Branching, in effect, permits a faster rate of self-pacing.
2. Contract Activity Packages	*A Contract Activity Package* includes:	
	1. Simply stated objectives that itemize exactly what the student is required to learn. 2. Multisensory resources that teach the information that the objectives indicate must be mastered. 3. A series of activities through which the information that has been mastered is used in a creative way.	4. A series of alternative ways in which creative activities developed by one student may be shared with one or more—but no more than six to eight—classmates. 5. At least three small-group techniques. 6. A pretest, a self-test, and a post-test.

Learning Style Characteristics to Which It Responds	Learning Style Characteristics to Which it Does Not Respond	Learning Style Characteristics to Which It Can Be Accommodated
Motivation, persistence, responsibility, and a need to work alone, a visually oriented student.	A lack of motivation, persistence, or responsibility; a need for flexibility or creativity; a need to work with peers or adults; auditory, tactual, or kinesthetic perceptual strengths.	Sound, light, temperature, and design; a need for intake, appropriate time of day, and a need for mobility.

Note: Where programmed learning sequences are accompanied by tapes, they will appeal to auditory learners; when they include films or filmstrips, they will reinforce the visually oriented student; when teachers design small-group techniques such as team learning, circle of knowledge, or brainstorming, peer-oriented students may develop an ability to use programs more effectively than if they use them exclusively as individual learners.

A need for sound and an informal design; motivation, persistence, and responsibility; a need to work either alone, with a friend or two, or with an adult, all perceptual strengths and weaknesses and the need for mobility.	None	Sound, light, temperature, and design; motivation, persistence, responsibility; sociological needs; perceptual strengths, intake, time of day, and the need for mobility.

Note: Contract Activity Packages respond to all learning style characteristics provided that (1) they are used correctly and (2) multisensory resources are developed as part of them.

Table 5 *(continued)*

Method or Resource	Brief Description
3. Instructional Packages	*Instructional Packages* are multisensory, self contained teaching units that have certain basic elements in in common: 1. Each package focuses on a single concept, e.g., time, adverbs, division of fractions, war as a human atrocity. 2. At least four senses are used to learn the contents, e.g., type-written script, audio tape, Kinesthetic Game, tactual activities. 3. Feedback and evaluation are built in, e.g., written tests, taped questions, self-correcting task cards—all with answers. 4. Learning is private and aimed at individual learning styles.
4. Task Cards and Learning Circles	*Task Cards:* Colored oak tag or cardboard rectangles that may be shape, color, or picture-coded for students to match words or questions with corresponding answers. *Learning Circles:* Oaktag circles divided into segments with questions on one side, responses on clothespins, and corresponding answers on the reverse side.
5. Tapes, Audio Cassette	*Tapes, Cassettes:* The recorded sound versions of printed or spoken material that should be learned.

Learning Style Characteristics to Which It Responds	Learning Style Characteristics to Which it Does Not Respond	Learning Style Characteristics to Which It Can Be Accommodated
A need for sound or structure; a need to work alone; all perceptual strengths.	A lack of responsibility; a need for peer or adult interactions.	Light, temperature, and design; motivation, persistence; intake, time of day, and mobility.

Note: Because of their multisensory activities, instructional packages are very effective with slow learners. Unless the curriculum is extremely challenging, they may be boring to high achievers.

Motivation, persistence, responsibility, and the need for structure; visual or tactual strengths.	A lack of motivation, persistence, responsibility, or a need for structure; auditory or kinesthetic strengths; a need for mobility.	Sound, light, temperature, and design; the need to work alone, with peers, or an adult; intake and time of day.
A need for sound; motivation, persistence, responsibility, and a need for structure; a need to work alone; auditory strengths.	A need for silence; a need to work with peers or an adult; visual, tactual or kinesthetic strengths, and a need for mobility.	Light, temperature, and design; intake and time of day.

All students, and certainly those with learning problems, need learning style analysis to identify how they learn best. Then, based on the findings, youngsters can be placed in the programs and provided the resources and methods that most adequately suit them. In much the same manner that physicians have replaced catch-all medicine show remedies, contemporary administrators and teachers will need to identify and respond to individual student differences.

Chapter 13

School Applications of the Learning Style Concept

James W. Keefe

John Henry Newman once said that nothing would be done if a man waited till he could do it so well that no one could find fault with it.

That is an essentially positive, forward looking notion.

Much of the historical quest for individualization in education has proceeded from such a perspective—that traditional education has persisted largely because few have tried for very long to make a serious change. In the United States, systematic programs of individualized instruction go back at least to the 1926 Winnetka (Illinois) Plan of Carleton Washbourne. The concept itself was suggested even earlier (before 1890) by Charles W. Eliot of Harvard. Its remote origins can be traced to Johann Heinrich Pestalozzi in 19th century Europe and perhaps to the 17th century educator John Amos Comenius.

Yet movements to individualize came and passed; hardly a ripple remained. And generally, no one had any regrets. Most of the attempts seemed faddish—the ebbs and tides of the school mainstream.

Even the great innovative surge of the 1960s was disappointing. Innovators of that decade felt secure in the conviction that *every human being is unique.* Accordingly, schools had to be designed for students, not for administrative convenience. Then came the financial crunch of the 1970s and test score declines. Some programs had to be cut back and others strengthened. Apparently, once again, the efforts at individualizing had been faulty; otherwise, why would test scores decline? It was time to rethink the premise.

Like most scenarios, this one has its measure of fact and fiction. Test scores declined for many reasons, chief among them that schools had moved their emphasis from building on basic skills to "providing alternatives." The baby had often been thrown out with the bath. It was certainly time to reestablish a solid foundation of reading, writing, and math skills before aspiring to more sophisticated goals. But, at the same time, if individualized education had failed, it was not that the concept had flaws, but that it had not been adequately tried. John Goodlad in his famous "look behind the classroom door" found that most innovations were honored in the breach rather than in the observance. Contemporary schools were long on good intentions and short in instructional strategy. Even the best of the new programs were disappointing because single-minded traditional techniques had been traded for single-minded innovative ones. The reality of individual differences demanded an approach founded on the fact of diversity. What was needed was more structure for some students and less for others, traditional programs for dependent learners and options for the independent types.

The goal of individualizing learning and instruction is an historical one, stretching back to early modern times. It is a *quest,* one which now finally may be within our grasp with the emergence of learning and teaching style. Previous efforts have been unsuccessful because they were based on a false epistemology, on a misunderstanding of how students learn. When we consider the dearth of professional knowledge about learning, the reliance largely on student or parental preference rather than on professional analysis, the futile attempts to innovate by making *all* students take independent study, or large group or whatever, is it any wonder that individualization has faltered? Now, however, we have the *beginning* of a science of human learning that can be applied in schools.

The concept of learning style revives the hope for authentic individualized education since it starts with the learner and then proceeds logically to a consideration of teaching and the learning environment. *An understanding of the way students learn is the door to educational improvement. And learning style diagnosis is the key to an understanding of student learning.*

School Implementation Alternatives

In our introductory chapter, we explored some 32 cognitive, affective and physiological learning styles. Some styles included for consideration are more tenuous in the research while others that may merit inclusion were omitted. Whatever the basis, the listing is tentative. Learning style is only now beginning to emerge from the laboratory and field-testing stages. To the practitioner, the view may be cloudy. The question arises: "What can the school staff do *now* to facilitate the identification of individual student learning style?"

A number of alternatives have been suggested by our contributing authors.

1. *Take a remedial approach.* Single out one or two learning styles that have readily available testing instrumentation and proceed in *therapeutic* fashion. Administer the test or inventory to those students who seem to have difficulty with the schools' dominant learning environment (e.g. traditional, modular, individualized, etc.). Look for general trends, i.e., whether most of the students having trouble exhibit similar learning profiles. A school opting for this approach might want to adopt one of the simpler methods. It could follow the Anderson/Bruce lead (Chapter 9) and use the *Group Embedded Figures Test* by Witkin to assess field independence/dependence or Rotter's *Internal/External Scale* to determine locus of control. (Anderson and Bruce found the Witkin and Rotter scales highly correlated in their study so one testing instrument may be enough for style identification). Students identified as more (or less) dependently oriented could be assigned more (or less) structured learning alternatives.

   Also helpful would be to look at differing physiological styles. Certainly sex-and health-related behaviors and environmental elements strongly affect student adjustment in school. Perhaps students experiencing difficulty are reacting to a biased learning environment where the approach is stacked against their predisposed physiological inclinations.

2. *Adopt a diagnostic approach.* Select one cognitive and one affective learning style or use one of the comprehensive inventories to identify the learning preferences of all students in the *entering class* of the school (grades 5, 7, 9 or 10). Test the transfer students. Then use the diagnostic data for student placement, goal setting and appropriate counseling.

   The Anderson/Bruce plan is workable at this level of implementation as well as Gregorc's Learning Preference Inventory (concrete/abstract modalities), Hunt's Paragraph Completion Method (conceptual level), SRI's Student Perceiver Interview (largely affective styles), the Dunn, Dunn and Price Learning Style Inventory or the Hill/Kusler Cognitive Mapping technique. Some of these evaluation techniques require special training, however, and school administrators will want to arrange for adequate staff development. Good basic sources of information are the references to be found at the end of this book, those pioneering schools already implementing learning style's programs, and workshops like the NASSP Institutes and SRI Perceiver Academies.

3. *Organize the entire school for advisement.* Utilize one or more of the evaluation techniques listed above and involve the entire staff in the processes of diagnosis, prescription, and evaluation. Enlist teachers and others as advisers (TAs) to assist in the diagnostic function. Staff development would be even more important in this kind of all-out effort. Further, there should be adequate time in the schedule and sufficient administrative support to make real advisement possible.

Proper attention to the diagnostic and planning function will significantly change the role of the guidance counselor. Professional counselors will be called upon to do more *educational* counseling. In preparing teachers for the diagnostic function, they will rejoin the instructional team in a new role. Where a system of teacher advisers already exists, TAs will play a more powerful role in the diagnostic process.

A school that adopts this approach acknowledges, at least implicitly, the validity of our school learning model. The only solid foundation for a responsive learning environment is careful diagnosis of individual learner traits followed by prescriptive/evaluative instructional techniques. Learning is not a one-way process but an interactive one. Diagnosis is meaningless without real learning options and a school will be inflexible unless teachers do something about it.

Learning Style Diagnosis

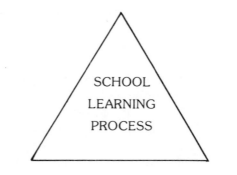

SCHOOL
LEARNING
PROCESS

Responsive
Learning Environment

Variability
in Teaching

David Cavanaugh in Chapter 11 recommends using the Learning Style Inventory (Dunn, Dunn and Price) for diagnosis directly related to instruction. Teachers who want to know how well students can adapt to alternative learning situations need practical data like that generated in the LSI. On the other hand, Cognitive Style Mapping appears to be more useful as a counseling tool in the hands of professional guidance personnel who assist students and staff in goal setting and academic trouble shooting. The same may well be true of Hunt's Paragraph Completion Method and the SRI Student Perceiver Interview.

Regardless of the approach, it will be important to acquaint parents with the meaning of learning styles and the practical implications for their own children.

Classroom Applications

Even when school organization cannot support a more comprehensive approach, classroom teachers can diagnose certain dimensions of learning style and modify instruction to accommodate individual differences. If no special testing budget is available, the teacher can begin *by observing students and answering a few diagnostic questions.* The following examples are derived from the cognitive style elements of perceptual modality, conceptual tempo, concept formation, and from motivational and physiological styles.[1]

PERCEPTUAL MODALITY. There are three basic ways by which people perceive reality: the visual (reading and viewing), the aural (hearing and speaking), and the psychomotor (doing). Perceptual preference seems to evolve for most students from psychomotor to visual and aural as the learner matures. A dominant preference usually forms early in life, however, and does not change radically.

We are not suggesting that learning style is a matter of student choice, but that preference develops from infancy almost subconsciously. In this perspective, the older pattern of "student options" can be replaced by a more thoughtful *prescription* or assignment of learning mode based upon analysis of learning style. The student is advised about his perceptual preferences and structured into certain learning alternatives depending upon his dominant style.

---

1. The cognitive material is based, in part, on "Individual Differences in Learning Styles" by Adaia Shumsky and "Learning Performance and Individual Differences: Prospective" by Len Sperry in *Learning Performance and Individual Differences* by Len Sperry. Glenview, Illinois: Scott, Foresman and Company, 1972.

A teacher alert to these preferences can arrange for flexibility in grouping, materials, and teaching style.

To assess dominant perceptual modality, the teacher can ask the following kinds of questions:

- What kind of learning activities does the learner seem to need? Handle the best?

- What seems to distract him?

- Does he remember better if he reads silently, reads and listens, listens only, or role plays an activity?

- Are his word associations and speech patterns more visual (imagery), aural (poetic) or behavioral (action-oriented)?

CONCEPTUAL TEMPO. Learners are different in the amount of time they need to get down to work and, then, to complete a learning task. They differ in tendency to work slowly with precision or quickly with abandon. In terms of tempo, people tend to be more or less reflective, more or less impulsive.

Schools interested in optimizing student pace and time-on-task should provide some practical form of individualized schedule. Students who need a great deal of structure to do good work should have close supervision and few distractions. Reflective students can be given much more flexibility in order to use resources in the community, to develop exploratory experiences, etc.

Teachers also will want to analyze their personal conceptual tempos in order to know how they affect their students' learning rates. Yardo and Kagan (1968) found that reflective teachers foster reflectiveness but impulsive teachers have little impact on students' tempo. Sperry (1972) suggests some interesting implications of this phenomenon:

> A teacher with a reflective tempo is likely to associate quickness with intelligence and will tend to reward impulsive learners who rapidly and accurately respond. The less able impulsive learner will then be at a disadvantage if speed of response is associated with inaccuracies in responding. This learner is being taught to value quickness, yet quickness may only enhance the learner's likelihood of failure.

Teachers can ask themselves these questions to diagnose conceptual tempo:

- Does the student work deliberately and accurately, or quickly and inaccurately?

- Does he work at the same pace for all tasks or vary his rate depending on the level of challenge?

- Does he aim to do good work or just finish an assignment?

CONCEPT FORMATION STRATEGIES. Some students grasp abstract concepts readily while others need concrete imagery to learn. Some use a broad, holistic approach to problem solving while others proceed small step by small step. Some learners are more analytic than others. One of the reasons that inductive, discovery-oriented approaches have not worked as a general methodology is that inquiry is most appropriate for the analytic learner. A lecture approach is better suited to the non-analytic type.

A teacher attempting to assess problem-solving preferences should determine:

- Does the learner see the world as complex or generally uncomplicated?

- Does he tend to define things abstractly or in concrete terms?

- Does he try to see the "big picture" before attempting a learning task, or does he begin immediately, working in narrow, linear fashion?

MOTIVATIONAL FACTORS. Affective learning styles are a product of learner personality, cultural environment, parental and peer pressures, and school influences. Students are motivated or not by the school itself, their teachers and the subjects they study. They are influenced by their general level of curiosity, their need for structure, desire for excellence, and simple personal interests. Indeed, knowing one's own learning style can be motivational in itself. As students understand their own learning proclivities and as they plan with teachers based on these tendencies, they will certainly be more motivated to learn.

At this point, we do not know, conclusively, which elements of motivation are most significant, but research by Lian-Hwang Chiu (1966) has distinguished five relatively independent factors. The teacher will want to ask questions based on these factors to derive a motivational profile:

- Does the student have a positive orientation toward learning? Does he show persistence and a high level of aspiration? Does he have positive feelings toward his academic self-concept and past performance?

- Does he manifest a need for academic recognition from teachers and peers?

- Does he fear failure and try to avoid it to a reasonable degree? (Underachievers may be too anxious or too phlegmatic to learn well).

- Is he curious, both about concepts and about things?

- Does he work when the teacher demands it, or his parents, or even his friends? Is he conforming to authority and peer influence?

PHYSIOLOGICAL FACTORS. The physical and the environmental have more influence on the learning process than most teachers and administrators are likely to admit. The way a student feels, whether he has had a nourishing breakfast, the time of day, the layout and atmosphere of the classroom, all these elements affect student performance. Teachers sensitive to the physiological influences on learning can provide a learning environment with useful options, provide for mobility or quiet and generally adapt classroom activities to individual differences.

Fortunately, physiological styles lend themselves readily to assessment by observation and simple questioning. Teachers can ask themselves and their students:

- Is this student performing to the level of his physical capabilities? Is his health reasonably good? Does he seem to get adequate nourishment at home and at school to work efficiently?

- Is he a morning or afternoon person? Is he able to function adequately during his "down time?"

- Can he sit still during the more demanding learning activities or is he inclined to fidget? Does he want to wander around?

- Does he require ordinary or high levels of lighting? Does noise seem to bother or help him?

- Are any of the males disadvantaged by the type and level of verbal tasks required? Are any of the females frustrated by the visual-spatial tasks?

Some Tentative Conclusions

The busy school administrator might well be inclined at this stage to sit back and let others explore the implications of learning style. Perhaps this would be a justifiable position if learning style were an ordinary notion. But it is not! As a foundation stone of the individualized education premise, learning style is the key to educational improvement in the decade of the 80s.

Learning style is much more than just another innovation. It is a fundamental new tool with which to work. It is a new way of looking at learning and instruction, a deeper and more profound view of the learner than known previously. It is a basic framework upon which a theory and practice of instruction can be built. It makes obsolete any single framework for teaching all students. All recent innovations, whether staff utilization, modular scheduling, independent study or fundamental education, must be rethought in the light of learning style.

It is nothing less than revolutionary to base instructional planning on an analysis of each student's traits. To do so moves education away from the traditional assembly-line, mass production model to a hand-crafted one. It also means, perhaps for the first time, that educators have more to work with than just the conventional wisdom about students and learning.

A practical perspective would be to take an easy first step, either schoolwide or within individual classrooms. Patricia Cross (1976) and others propose some evident possibilities:

1. Establish a systematic program of inservice on learning styles for teachers, students, and parents.

2. Work toward a more flexible learning environment in the school. No method of instruction works for all students. Provide alternatives. Avoid systematically biasing instruction in favor of any one learning style.

3. Make certain that basic skills instruction reflects some systematic form of student learning styles diagnosis.

4. Concentrate on better student advisement and guidance. The learning style concept is relatively value-fair and has great potential for academic program planning and career counseling.

5. Keep an open mind. Much is known already about cognitive styles, less in a systematic way about affective and physiological styles. The research is incomplete but growing rapidly. A few schools have done a great deal; others must accept the challenge.

Educators must begin to base programs on the individual differences that exist among learners rather than on the assumption that everybody learns in the same way. The concept of learning style views individual differences as normative and accepts them as challenge rather than liability.

Learning style diagnosis opens the door to placing individualized instruction on a more rational basis. It gives the most powerful leverage yet available to educators to analyze, motivate, and assist students in school. As such, it is the foundation of a truly modern approach to education.

Representative Learning Style Instruments

General

Cognitive Style Mapping Inventory by Joseph E. Hill (1964). Compiled and revised edition for computer scoring, East Lansing High School, East Lansing, Michigan (1975).

Learning Style Inventory (LSI) by Rita Dunn, Kenneth Dunn and Gary E. Price (1978), available from Price Systems, Box 3271, Lawrence, Kansas 66044. (Computer scored only)

SRI Student Perceiver Interview. Training leading to certification offered in designated cities. Information from Selection Research, Inc., 2546 South 48th Street, Lincoln, Nebraska 68506. (Primarily affective styles)

Cognitive

Group Embedded Figures Test (GEFT) by Philip K. Oltman, Evelyn Raskin and Herman A. Witkin (1971) available from Consulting Psychologists Press, Inc., 577 College Avenue, Palo Alto, California 94306. (Field independence/dependence)

Matching Familiar Figures Test (MFF) by Jerome Kagan published in "Impulsive and Reflective Children", *Learning and the Educational Process* by J. Krumboltz. Chicago: Rand, McNally, 1965, pp. 133-161. (Conceptual tempo)

Schematizing Test by R.W. Gardner et al. published in "Cognitive Control: A Study of Individual Consistencies in Cognitive Behavior." *Psychological Issues,* 1959, Vol. 1, No. 4. (Leveling/sharpening)

Affective

Internal-External (I-E) Scale by Julian B. Rotter published in "Generalized Expectancies for Internal Versus External Control of Reinforcements." *Psychological Monographs,* Vol. 80, No. 10, 1966, pp. 1-28 (Locus of Control)

Paragraph Completion Method, David E. Hunt in *Assessing Conceptual Level by the Paragraph Completion Method* by D.E. Hunt, et al., Toronto: Ontario Institute for Studies in Education (252 Bloor Street West), 1978.

Selected References

Ball, Samuel, Editor, *Motivation in Education*. New York: Academic Press, Inc., 1977.

Biehler, Robert F., *Psychology Applied to Teaching*. Second Edition. Boston: Houghton Mifflin Company, 1974.

Bloom, Benjamin S., *Human Characteristics and School Learning*. New York: McGraw-Hill Book Company, 1976.

Bonneau, L.R., "An Interview for Selecting Teachers," Unpublished Doctoral Dissertation, University of Nebraska, 1956.

Bugelski, B.R., *The Psychology of Learning Applied to Teaching,* Second Edition. Indianapolis: The Bobbs-Merrill Company, Inc., 1971.

Bruce, S.W., "A Study of Cognitive Style and Locus of Control in Relation to Student Achievement and Student Preference for Selected Modes of Instruction." Unpublished Doctoral Dissertation, University of Southern California, 1979.

Chall, Jeanne S. and Allan F. Mersky, eds. *Education and the Brain*. Seventy-seventh Yearbook of the National Society for the Study of Education, Part II. Chicago: University of Chicago Press, 1978.

Cronbach, Lee J. and Richard E. Snow, *Aptitudes and Instructional Methods*. New York: Irvington Publishers, Inc. (Halsted Press), 1977.

Cross, K. Patricia, *Accent on Learning*. San Francisco: Jossey-Bass Publishers, 1977.

Davis, J., *Technical Report #32: Concept Identification as a Function of Cognitive Style, Complexity, and Training Procedure*. Madison, Wisconsin: Center for Cognitive Learning, 1967.

De Cecco, John P., *The Psychology of Learning and Instruction: Educational Psychology*. Englewood Cliffs, New Jersey: Prentice-Hall, Inc., 1968.

Dodge, G.W., "Aptitude for Positive Teacher-Pupil Rapport," Unpublished Doctoral Dissertation, University of Nebraska, 1964.

Domino, George, "Interactive Effects of Achievement Orientation and Teaching Style on Academic Achievement," ACT Research Report No. 39, 1970, pp. 1-9.

Dunn, Rita and Kenneth Dunn, "Learning As a Criterion for Placement in Alternative Programs," *Phi Delta Kappan*, December 1974, pp. 275-279.

Dunn, Rita and Kenneth Dunn, *Educator's Self-Teaching Guide to Individualizing Instructional Programs*. West Nyack, New York: Parker Publishing Company, Inc., 1975.

Dunn, Rita and Kenneth Dunn, "Finding the Best Fit: Learning Styles, Teaching Styles," *NASSP Bulletin*, Vol. 59, October 1975, pp. 37-49.

Dunn, Rita and Kenneth Dunn, *Administrator's Guide to New Programs for Faculty Management and Evaluation.* West Nyack, N.Y.: Parker Publishing Co., Inc., 1977.

Dunn, Rita and Kenneth Dunn, *Teaching Students Through Their Individual Learning Styles.* Reston, Virginia: Reston Publishing Company, Inc. (Prentice-Hall Co.), 1978.

Dunn, Rita and Gary Price, "Identifying the Learning Style Characteristics of Gifted Children," *The Gifted Child Quarterly,* National Association for Gifted Children (in press).

Farr, Beatrice J., "Individual Differences in Learning: Predicting Ones More Effective Learning Modality," Unpublished Doctoral Dissertation, Catholic University of America, 1971.

Goldberg, Miriam L., *Research on the Talented.* New York: Teachers College, Columbia University, 1965.

Gregorc, Anthony F., "Learning/Teaching Styles: Potent Forces Behind Them." *Educational Leadership,* Vol. 36, No. 4, January 1979, pp. 234-36.

Hawkins, George, "Motivation and Individual Learning Styles," *Engineering Education,* Vol. 64, No. 6, March 1974, pp. 407-411.

Hill, Joseph E., et al. *Personalizing Educational Programs Utilizing Cognitive Style Mapping.* Bloomfield Hills, Michigan: Oakland Community College, 1971.

Hill, Joseph E., *The Educational Sciences,* Revised Edition. Bloomfield Hills, Michigan: Oakland Community College, 1976.

Holzman, P.S. and Klein, G.S., "Cognitive System—Principles of Leveling and Sharpening: Individual Differences in Assimilation Effects in Visual Time Error." *Journal of Psychology,* Vol. 37, 1954, pp. 105-122.

Hunt, D.E., *Matching Models in Education.* Toronto: Ontario Institute for Studies in Education, 1971.

Hunt, D.E., L.F. Butler, J.E. Noy and M.E. Rosser. *Assessing Conceptual Level by the Paragraph Completion Method.* Toronto: Ontario Institute for Studies in Education, 1978.

Hunt, David E., "Conceptual Level Theory and Research As Guides to Educational Practice." *Interchange,* Vol. 8, No. 4, 1977-78, pp. 78-90.

Joyce, Bruce and Marsha Weil, *Models of Teaching.* Englewood Cliffs, N.J.: Prentice-Hall, Inc., 1972.

Kagan, Jerome and John Wright, *Basic Cognitive Processes in Children.* Lafayette, Indiana: Child Development Publications, 1963.

Kagan, Jerome, "Reflection-Impulsivity: The Generality and Dynamics of Conceptual Tempo," *Journal of Abnormal Psychology,* Vol. 71, 1966, pp. 17-24.

Kogan, Nathan. "Educational Implications of Cognitive Styles," in Lesser, Gerald S. (ed.), *Psychology and Educational Practice*. Glenview, Illinois: Scott, Foresman and Co., 1972.

Leslie, Herold P., et al., *Field Sensitive and Field Independent Teaching Strategies: New Approaches to Bilingual Bicultural Education, No. 5.* HEW sponsored teaching manual from the Dissemination Center for Bilingual Bicultural Education, Austin, Texas, 1974, 25 p.

Luria, A.R., *The Working Brain,* B. Haigh, translator. New York: Basic Books, Inc., 1973.

Maccoby, Eleanor E. and Carol N. Jacklin, "What We Know and Don't Know About Sex Differences," *Psychology Today,* December, 1974, pp. 109-112.

Marcus, Lee, "A Comparison of Selected 9th Grade Male and Female Students' Learning Styles," *The Journal,* School Administrators Association of New York State, Vol. 7, No. 3, January 1977, pp. 27-28.

Marcus, Lee, "Learning Style and Ability Grouping Among Seventh Grade Students," *The Clearing House,* Vol. 8, No. 52, April 1979, pp. 377-80.

Martin, Michael Kenneth, "Effects of the Interaction Between Students' Learning Styles and High School Instructional Environments," Unpublished Doctoral Dissertation, University of Oregon, 1977.

McGuinness, Diane, "How Schools Discriminate Against Boys," *Human Nature,* February 1979, pp. 82-88.

McKenney, James L. and Peter G.W. Keen. "How Managers' Minds Work." *Harvard Business Review,* Vol. 53, No. 3, 1974, pp. 79-90.

Messick, Samuel and Associates, *Individuality in Learning.* San Francisco: Jossey-Bass Publishers, 1976.

Nelson, Karen H., "Cognitive Styles and Sex Roles in Teaching-Learning Processes." Paper presented at Annual Convention of the American Psychological Association, San Francisco, CA, 1977, 18 p.

Niederwerfer, M.B., "The Relationship Between Selected Individual Differences and the Ease With Which Teachers Change Their Strategy." Unpublished Doctoral Dissertation, Cornell University, 1975.

Ramirez, Manuel III, et al., *Introduction to Cognitive Styles: New Approaches to Bilingual Bicultural Education, No. 3.* HEW sponsored teaching manual from the Dissemination Center for Bilingual Bicultural Education, Austin, Texas, 1974, 22 p.

Rotter, Julian B., "Generalized Expectancies for Internal Versus External Control of Reinforcements," *Psychological Monographs,* Vol. 80, No. 10, 1966, pp. 1-28.

Rotter, J.B., "External Control and Internal Control," *Psychology Today,* Vol. 5, June 1971, pp. 37-42.

Sperry, Len, *Learning Performance and Individual Differences.* Glenview, Illinois: Scott, Foresman and Company, 1972.

Steele, Joe M., Ernest A. House, Stephan D. Lapan and Thomas Kerins, "Cognitive and Affective Patterns of Emphasis in Gifted and Average Illinois Classes," *Exceptional Children,* Vol. 37, 1971, pp. 757-59.

Thornell, J.G., "Individual Differences in Cognitive Styles and the Guidance Variable in Instruction," *The Journal of Experimental Education,* Vol. 42, 1973, pp. 59-63.

Treffinger, Donald J., "Teaching for Self-Directed Learning: A Priority for the Gifted and Talented," *Gifted Child Quarterly,* Vol. 19, 1975, pp. 46-59.

Weisberger, Robert A., *Perspectives in Individualized Learning.* Chicago: Peacock Publishers, Inc., 1971.

Witkin, H.A., et al., *Personality Through Perception.* New York: Harper and Brothers, 1954.

Witkin, H.A., P.K. Oltman, E. Raskin and S.A. Karp. *A Manuel for the Embedded Figures Test.* Palo Alto, Calif.: Consulting Psychologists Press, 1971.

Witkin, H.A., *Cognitive Style and the Teaching-Learning Process.* American Educational Research Association Audiotape, 1974.

Zytkoskee, Adrian, et al., "Delay of Gratification and Internal Versus External Control Among Low Socio-Economic Adolescents." Paper presented at Southeastern Psychological Convention, Atlanta, GA, 1969, 14 p.